BERLITZ®

1988/1989 Edition

By the staff of Berlitz Guides
A Macmillan Company

9th Printing
1988/1989 Edition

COSTA
BRAVA

How to use our guide

- All the practical information, hints and tips that you will need before and during the trip start on page 98.

- For general background, see the sections The Costa Brava and the Catalans, p. 6, and A Brief History, p. 10.

- All the sights to see are listed between pages 17 and 72. Our own choice of sights most highly recommended is pinpointed by the Berlitz traveller symbol.

- Entertainment, nightlife and all other leisure activities are described between pages 73 and 89, while information on restaurants and cuisine is to be found on pages 90 to 97.

- Finally, there is an index at the back of the book, pp. 126–128.

Although we make every effort to ensure the accuracy of all the information in this book, changes occur incessantly. We cannot therefore take responsibility for facts, prices, addresses and circumstances in general that are constantly subject to alteration. Our guides are updated on a regular basis as we reprint, and we are always grateful to readers who let us know of any errors, changes or serious omissions they come across.

Text and photography: Ken Welsh; picture p. 70: PRISMA/Etienne
We wish to thank Joanna Pencarska and the Spanish National Tourist Office, particularly Mercedes Martín Bartolomé, for their valuable assistance.
Cartography: 🔵 Falk-Verlag, Hamburg

4

Contents

Maps

The Costa Brava and the Catalans

If ever one small part of the planet was blessed with everything, this is surely it. Facing the Mediterranean, flanked to the north by the mighty Pyrenees, the Costa Brava offers sandy beaches, hidden coves, offshore islands, charming fishing villages, imposing castles with a backdrop of magnificent mountains and a first-rate climate. It forms part of the Catalonian province of Girona, and is a region of history and art, of cathedrals and achievements, of alternately lush and harsh scenery and, to top it all, the best skiing in Spain.

To the seafaring Catalans, this particular strip of the coast was always known as *brava,* a term with a whole range of meanings: wild, savage, dangerous, craggy, stormy, steep. But it was the Catalan poet, Ferrán Agulló, who, in 1908, first officially coined the name for the coast as a geographical entity running from Banyuls (just over the border in France) down to the estuary of the Tordera.

To find out just how wild, geographically speaking, the Costa Brava is, take an hour's drive around the hairpin bends above the cliffs of the northern or southern extremes of the coast. And even then you've only had a glimpse; the rest is hidden…

A droll little Girona joke asks, "In how many countries of the world do they speak Spanish?" Answer: "Well, now, they speak it in Galicia, the Basque country, in Catalonia…" A very wry joke, but it helps to explain Spain's fascination. For Spain is many nations under one flag, and Catalonia is one of them.

Spanish is, in fact, one of two languages spoken in Catalonia. The people of Girona, and the other three provinces of Catalonia, are bilingual. They speak Catalan, a derivative of Latin, along with (and often better than) the national language of Spain, Castilian. Catalan or its dialects are spoken from the French Pyrenees to Valencia, in the Balearic Islands and, surprisingly, in parts of Sardinia—a reminder of Catalonia's great medieval kingdom. Catalan is today official language of Catalonia on a par with Castilian.

You'll often be reminded that the Catalans are a race apart, as different from the Andalusians or Basques as the Welsh and Scots are from the English. They are acutely aware of their own history and culture.

Unlike the Spanish stereotype, the Catalans are dynamic, canny and industrious. This may account for their reputation elsewhere in Spain as mercenary and uncompromising. Catalonia's best reply is the roster of outstanding artists who have emerged during a century desperately short of talent in other parts of the country. Caught between the two worlds of Europe and Iberia, Catalonia has been

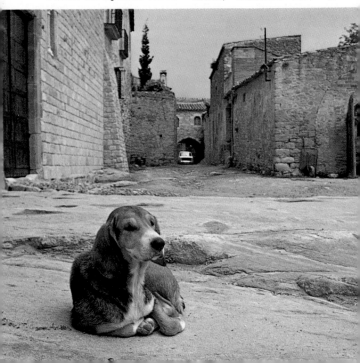

able to absorb the best of both and produce giants such as Joan Miró, Salvador Dalí and, something of an adopted son, Picasso. In architecture the genius was Gaudí; in music, Casals.

Music is important in the lives of the Catalans. They sing in choirs, play in bands and dance the *sardana*. This gracious, courtly dance is as essentially Catalan as flamenco is Andalusian. And it is a living part of the culture, not a folklore oddity dragged out of the cupboard to entertain the tourists. The *sardana* bridges the generation gap; young and old join hands to dance it every week in resorts up and down the Costa Brava.

"People interpret the closed circle of the *sardana* as a symbol of our unity *against* the outside world," goes the Catalan explanation. "But if anyone, even a foreigner, touches the circle, it opens to accept him. *That* is a symbol of our willingness to embrace anyone who attempts to understand us."

Your desire to understand the Catalans—if not necessarily to be embraced by them—can only be heightened by the dramatic surroundings of the Costa Brava. But as you enjoy their scenery and hearty food and wine, as you tour their archaeological wonders and religious shrines, as you take advantage of the sports and nightlife and shopping... try not to envy them. After all, they were here first.

Left: *Old stones and lazy hound in Peratallada show town's easy pace. Typical feature of the Costa Brava is its jagged coastline (beware of twisting roads), as here near Tossa.*

A Brief History

Beneath the stone, sand and soil of the Costa Brava lurks the treasure of history. Digging, scraping and deducing, archaeologists have pieced together a new insight into Catalonia's ancient heritage.

Their most dramatic success has been the excavation of twin Greek and Roman cities at Empuries (Ampurias), where the Greeks had set up a very important trading post. Another impressive discovery, inland from L'Estartit, revealed a 5th-century B.C. Celtiberian city at Ullastret.

The Celtiberians were the descendants of northern Celtic tribes who invaded the peninsula and settled down with the earlier arrivals, the Iberians.

Though several Mediterranean peoples traded and colonized on Spain's shores, the first to make any real impact on Spanish history were the ambitious and warlike Carthaginians, arch-rivals of the Romans for Mediterranean supremacy. Hannibal, the military genius of Carthage, saw Catalonia as the gateway to victory. He marched his elephants through Girona Province as he prepared to invade Rome during the Second Punic War, but failed, and Rome enfolded Spain into its ever-expanding empire. The brave Celtiberians resisted for two whole centuries, but around 20 B.C., the last part of the peninsula (Galicia) was finally subdued and declared a Roman province.

Rome brought political stability and an advanced culture to Spain. During the six centuries of occupation, the Romans built cities and roads, inaugurated government and law, and provided the base for the Spanish and Catalan languages. The colony, in turn, made its contribution to the thriving civilization of Rome: the philosopher Seneca, the poet Martial and the emperors Trajan and Hadrian, all were born in Spain.

But as the unwieldy empire entered its decline, successive waves of intruders chipped away at the Roman edifice. Spain was overrun by Vandals and Visigoths. Corruption and intrigue in the 300-year Visigothic occupation left the kingdom defenceless in the face of Spain's most momentous event.

In A.D. 711, the Moors of North Africa invaded across the Straits of Gibraltar. They defeated the Visigothic defenders at Tarifa and within ten years had conquered most of the country. Then, crossing the Pyrenees, they pushed into France until the Frankish general, Charles Martel, turned them back at Poitiers in 732.

The Moors installed their religion and culture in Spain, but Christian resistance never died. The battle to expel Islam see-sawed for centuries before

The 'Catholic Monarchs' Ferdinand and Isabella united Spain in 1492.

the ultimate triumph of the Catholic Monarchs, Ferdinand and Isabella.

In the early stages of the struggle, Charlemagne, the Frankish warrior-king, expelled the Moors from Girona and Barcelona. He integrated these territories into what was called the Spanish March, a buffer zone between the Christian and Muslim power bases.

The first hero of Catalonia emerged in a skirmish between the Frankish forces and the Moors. His name was Wifredo el Velloso (Guifredo Pelio in Catalan), meaning Wilfred the Hairy. The noble Wilfred threw his support behind a Frankish king who was his opposite number in more ways

10th-century Monastery of Sant Pere de Roda, north Costa Brava, was an important religious centre.

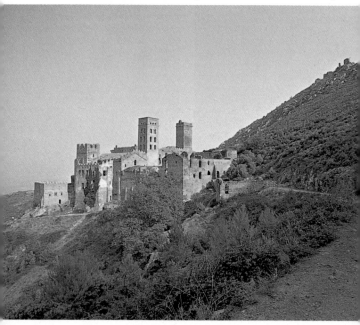

than one, Charles the Bald. When Wilfred fell wounded, the legend goes, the king asked what reward he desired. The request—independence for Barcelona—was granted. The year was 878.

The Golden Age

In the Middle Ages, Catalonia became strong commercially, politically and intellectually. Count Ramón Berenguer I of Barcelona drew up a sort of constitution, the *Usatges,* in 1060. Ramón Berenguer III (1096–1131) expanded trade alliances. But the Berenguer dynasty's greatest coup took place at the church altar when Ramón IV (1131–62) married the daughter of the King of Aragon, creating the joint kingdom of Catalonia and Aragon.

In Catalonia's heyday, the combined Crown was scarcely challenged in the Mediterranean. At one time Catalonia controlled outposts in Greece, Italy, Sicily, Sardinia and Corsica. Shipyards worked overtime to expand the Catalan merchant fleet; the Crown wrote a code of maritime law; and an enterprising group of merchants founded a marine insurance company.

Conquest—more economic than military—was by no means everything. This was the era of great architecture and art: original churches with vast naves and tall, slim columns and the astonishing sculptures and paintings which glorified them. And Catalonia's scholars and philosophers prospered.

The most significant nuptials in three centuries united Ferdinand, Prince of Aragon, and Isabella of Castile in 1469. Their combined kingdom began the final conquest of the tenacious Moors, culminating in the capture of Granada in 1492. The Catholic Monarchs supervised two other historic events of the same year. They expelled the Jews from Spain. And they sent Columbus on his voyage to America.

The Columbus project and other adventures far afield had ironic effects on Catalonia. As Spain entered its Golden Age, all eyes now turned to the wealth of the New World, stripping the Mediterranean trade routes of much of their importance. And, in the interprovince rivalries, the Catalonians found themselves relegated to a second-class position in favour of Castile. Catalans were even forbidden access to the New World territories. The great new commercial centres were Cádiz and Seville. **13**

Times of Troubles

The uncountable riches the Conquistadors shipped home from America drastically strengthened Spain's position in European politics. But the seeds of disaster were planted. Spain's gold drained away in endless wars in Italy and Holland. The demoralizing defeat of the Invincible Armada in 1588 brought further ruin. Each military adventure and commodatingly recognized the region as an independent state. The revolt of the Catalans raged for more than a decade. Spain won. In defeat, Catalonia managed to preserve its treasured local laws, but under allegiance to the Spanish Crown.

In the War of the Spanish Succession—really a struggle between France and the rest of Europe—Catalonia sided with

Girona's medieval walls helped to defend city against many a siege.

each new king seemed worse than the last.

In Catalonia, the discontent seethed against Philip IV, flaming into open rebellion in 1640. Louis XIII of France ac- the loser, Archduke Charles of Austria. Battles flared, cities were besieged. With the triumph of the Bourbon king, Philip V, the Catalonians were punished once more. The parliament was disbanded, and the Catalan language was banned from official use.

Along with the rest of Spain, Catalonia counted as little more than a satellite of France.

In the Peninsular War of 1808–14, which the Spaniards call the War of Independence, Catalonia fared badly yet again. The French quickly conquered Barcelona, but Girona underwent a nine-month siege. A French army of 35,000 finally breached the walls of the starving city with mines. Eventually, with the aid of their new British allies led by the Duke of Wellington, Spain won its independence.

The legitimate monarchy may have been restored, but Spain now plunged headlong into a century of disastrous power struggles. Overseas, Spain's American colonies revolted and gained independence. The last Spanish possessions—Cuba, Puerto Rico and the Philippines—were eventually lost when the Americans intervened in the year 1898.

Following an embarrassing defeat by local rebels in Morocco, Alfonso XIII, in 1923, accepted a general, Primo de Rivera, as dictator of Spain. Seven years later the general fell. Neither reform nor maintenance of order seemed possible. In 1931, the king himself went into exile as anti-royalist sentiment grew.

National elections favoured the Republicans, who advocated Socialist and anti-clerical policies. As conservative resistence began to crystallize, Catalonia was proclaimed an autonomous republic. This was the first time in more than two centuries that home rule had been achieved.

The Civil War

Confusion and disorder were growing in Spain. The conflict between left and right became more irreconcilable. Spain's youngest general, Francisco Franco, came to the head of a military insurrection in 1936. The whole world watched the three-year struggle; outside forces helped to prolong it. Franco, with the Nationalists, Falangists and Monarchists, could call upon the tanks and planes of Germany and Italy. The Republicans, a shaky coalition of Socialists, Communists and Anarchists, received help from Moscow and the volunteer International Brigades.

Military reverses forced the Republicans to move their capital from Valencia to Barcelona in late 1937, where there had already been an outbreak of bitter fighting be- **15** tween two factions of the Republican side, Anarchists and Communists. There followed repeated bombings of Barcelona by Italian planes based on Majorca and a year of hardship for the population. The city fell at last in January, 1939, and Catalonia was again absorbed into Spain—four provinces out of the nation's 50. Within two months, the Civil War, in which not far from half a million Spaniards were killed, was over.

Modern Times

Spain managed to stay on the sidelines in the Second World War. In the postwar years, the tough law-and-order regime of Franco set in motion the nation's recovery. Then came the phenomenon of mass tourism, with profound effects on the economy and the people.

Franco's designated successor, the grandson of Alfonso XIII, was enthroned on the death of the dictator in 1975. To the dismay of Franco's followers, King Juan Carlos I flung open the gates to full

Going about day-to-day tasks in a typical old Catalonian village. Right: Winding roads of Pyrenean foothills hug coast by Portbou.

parliamentary democracy. After decades of repression, the language and culture of Catalonia flourished anew, and regional autonomy was granted. Spain returned to the mainstream of Europe.

Although life has undergone drastic changes, Spain's perennial advantages—scenic beauty, fine climate, warm welcome—are as abundant and inviting as ever.

Where to Go

To most Spaniards, the Costa Brava begins in Blanes north of Barcelona and ends at Portbou on the French frontier; but to most outsiders it's the other way round, so we begin our survey heading south from the French border, with short inland excursions where desirable.

The Northern Reach

Where Spain meets France, the formidable Pyrenees roll down to meet the sea, and one of the most spectacular coastlines of the whole Mediterranean begins: nearly 125 miles of dramatic cliffs, hidden coves, a myriad of villages interspersed with broad and sandy beaches.

Little wonder that the Costa Brava has earned such a reputation: a pure blue sea barely ruffled by a few white specks, seen against a protective green wall of huge pines, perfectly shaped like open umbrellas and contrasting with the ochre earth. Gnarled olive trees, the

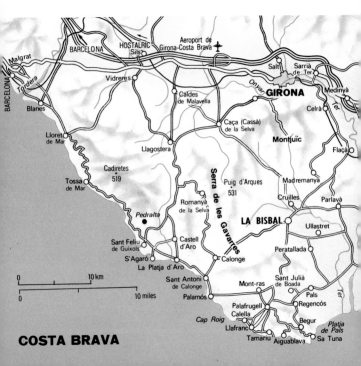

COSTA BRAVA

pita (century plant), with its characteristic tall shoot in the middle, and the tortuous cork trees add to the extraordinary symphony of colour.

Hunched round a small bay below the lonely frontier post lies PORTBOU, a fishing village which enjoyed a brief period of notoriety early this century as a haven for smug-glers coming and going be-tween France and Spain. A strait-laced border town now, it is fondly remembered by countless motorists as their first taste of Spain—and per-haps their first swim in the pretty CALA PETITA.

Southwards the road twists and turns like tangled string threading its way through the

Pyrenean foothills until a dozen long kilometres later it finds LLANÇÀ, now almost joined to its port, Port de Llançà. This quiet bay with its scorched and barren mountain backdrop was famed in particular for its rugged fishermen—said to be the most skilful on the whole Brava coast—and for its tasty wines.

As so often on the Costa Brava, town and port were in former times separate, for Llançà, a thriving commercial harbour exporting wine and olives to France and Italy, was constantly being attacked by pirates. The town also developed a prosperous marble industry. Today, however, it is in the import business, enticing sun-starved Northerners to come and enjoy the delights of its beaches. Facing north, it is slightly cooler in summer than the rest of the Costa Brava, and its quarter mile of shingly beach and the shallow waters attract many tourists in search of peace and quiet.

Naked hills shield **El Port de la Selva** (8 km. beyond) from icy winds (the *tramontana*) whipping down from the Pyrenees in winter. But these same hills were once so densely wooded (the name means "port of the woods") that the only easy access was by sea.

This natural protection offered safety to prehistoric communities; flint knives, pottery and over 70 Iron Age graves have been unearthed in the area around Punta del Pi.

A few treacherous motorcraft have crept in among the fishing boats in the pretty natural port, closed in by the dock. The town's site, clustered round its bay and protected by the towering mountains behind, inspires its reputation as the capital of this northern stretch of the Costa Brava.

As with Llançà, El Port de la Selva has its "twin" town 2 kilometres inland. LA SELVA DE MAR huddles in a small valley not visible from the sea, and its main activity used to be farming; its port grew up later when the danger of pirate attacks had abated. Apart from its charm, La Selva de Mar serves as departure point for the **Monastery of Sant Pere de Roda.**

Two hours' hard walking takes a visitor to the top of bleak Mount Vedera (over 2,000 feet); you won't regret your exertions when you see the impressive ruins of a 10th-century fortified monastery. Benedictine monks enlarged it and reconstructed existing foundations to make this the most influential ecclesiastical centre in the region.

This landmark of Catalonian Romanesque architecture, abandoned in the 18th century, is being extensively restored. The noble monastery, set against the arid landscape with the sea and El Port de la Selva far below, makes an unforgettable sight.

Mount Vedera, the last Pyrenean foothill to reach the coast, also provides a suitably mysterious setting for ruins of the Castell de Sant Salvador (Castle of the Holy Saviour).

For those who prefer to come by car, a difficult road of bumps and potholes leaves from VILAJUIGA, 9 kilometres away.

Plenty of fun and sun for all on town beach at El Port de la Selva.

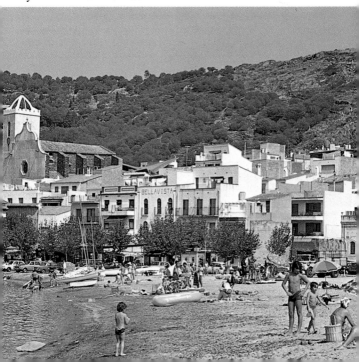

⚓ Cadaqués

If El Port de la Selva is "capital" of the northern reaches of the Costa Brava and Roses that of the southern stretch, Cadaqués rules in splendid isolation over the Peninsula of Cap de Creus to the east.

The road linking El Port de la Selva with Cadaqués, 12 kilometres away, is wearying, with few signs of life or even vegetation. Yet Cadaqués is

one of the most hospitable and picturesque of all the spots on the Costa Brava.

Coming as it does at the end of an intense, desolate drive, the sudden sight of this charming town is something of a miracle. On a steep hillside, dazzling white houses with red roofs climb towards the massive church through straggling cobbled alleyways. At the harbour, cafés and restaurants beside the promenade look over the small bay where a few fishing boats keep up the image of a fishing village while water-skiers perform in front.

Cadaqués has had a long, eventful history, marked in particular by pirate raids, which has no doubt given the people their reputation as indomitable characters, self-assured and independent (and the coast's most skilful smugglers). The worst raid of all came with Barbarossa (Red Beard), who in 1543 sacked the town and burned the original church. The present church, built in the 17th century, has a remarkable Baroque altarpiece by Pau Costa.

Other regular invaders were the French; in 1285, the town recorded its first French intrusion and during the Peninsular War, its last (official) one. But even today Cadaqués is invaded every summer by the French, along with holidaymakers of a dozen nationalities. They tend to return regularly, swearing that this town with its pleasant rhythm of life and exceptionally clear light is the prettiest of all; one only has to see the number of easels planted everywhere to realize that it is a real artist's town.

The fame of Cadaqués has certainly been enhanced by the reputation and antics of the surrealist painter Salvador Dalí and his wife Gala, who settled in 1929 in **Portlligat,**

2 kilometres beyond Cadaqués. In that year, Dalí bought a one-roomed fisherman's house. Afterwards he acquired adjoining houses and re-designed them for the attractive Daliesque enclave to be seen down by the port today.

Many of Dalí's works uncannily reflect the pervading spirit of this strange region. "Here", he once said, "the mornings are of a savage and bitter gaiety and the evenings are often tinged with a morbid melancholy". Much of the jagged coastline is difficult to reach except by boat. Cadaqués itself and the road running round the bay are often choked with cars.

Cadaqués, with its dazzling white houses, rules in splendid solitude over the Cap de Creus Peninsula.

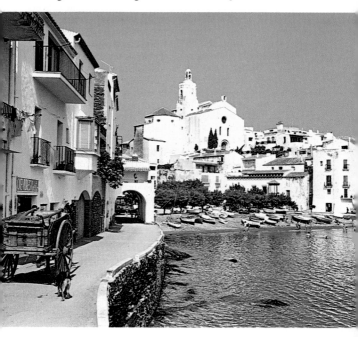

Roses

On the southern part of the Cap de Creus, at Roses, 15 kilometres beyond Cadaqués, begins a new type of Costa Brava: hospitable horizons, long, open beaches, expanses of flat country and the fertile Empordà plain behind. Roses, from its original nucleus on the peninsula, spreads every year further down the lovely curve of the Golf de Roses, offering mile after mile of gently sloping sandy beaches. The setting is superb: on one side, the bay with its incredibly blue waters and, in the background, the lofty Pyrenees, at their most beautiful in winter and spring when the sun glitters on the snow on the peaks and reflects off the deep blue sea. It had long been a coastal favourite of the inhabitants of Figueres, 18 kilometres inland; the seemingly unending apartment blocks testify to its success.

Its popularity isn't new. The Greeks set up a trading post here (some claim that the name Roses comes from Rhodes) and even earlier megalithic monuments have been found at Creu d'en Cobertella. From Roses in 1354, in Catalonia's heyday, a fleet of 300 ships set sail to quell a revolt in Sardinia. In the 14th century, the town grew rich on the coral trade, and in 1543 Charles I built the massive, star-shaped fortress, La Ciutadella, as a measure against marauders. Despite this precaution, during the Peninsular War Roses was taken by the French, who dismantled its fortifications piece by piece; you can still see the ruins today.

Roses is famous for more than its outstanding beaches: thanks to the contortions of the coast's geography, the **port** faces due west; it has the most glorious sunsets on the whole Costa Brava. The reflection of the setting sun in the windows of the town is a memorable sight, with the distant peaks of the Garrotxa range beyond bathed in orange and red.

Not to be missed either is the arrival at about 6 in the evening of the fishing fleet, still a mainstay of the local economy. The return of the *vaques* to the perfect natural harbour formed by the Bay of Roses never fails to move a visitor. Watch them auction the seafood on little round trays (the fish here are some of the tastiest on the whole coast).

If you find the long, flat beach too unexciting and require more adventurous

Lone sailing boat on a placid sea adds to dramatic sunset off Roses.

bathing, explore the coastline to the north of Roses—one intriguing *cala* (cove) after another.

Eight kilometres outside Roses lies the large new residential and holiday complex of EMPURIA-BRAVA, set off between the rivers Salines and Muga. To many—but not all—it is the successful realization of the concept of an integrated holiday centre, incorporating facilities for all seaside and other outdoor activities, in a harmonious architectural ensemble. A maritime promenade skirts a fine white beach over a mile long. There's a yacht harbour and underwater-fishing club, and boat-supply shops with everything any skipper could want. A network of canals leads inland so that boats can be moored at the backdoor of the more luxurious quayside homes. The housing is low-key and cubic. Hotels, shopping centres, an observation tower (mirador), a shooting range, discotheques, tennis courts, an aero-club with its airfield—these are just a sample of what's to be found—plus the fine bathing on the beach in front.

Inland from Roses

In this low-lying coastal area, the sea has abandoned some towns, leaving them high and dry when the region silted up. CASTELLÓ D'EMPÚRIES is a case of a stranded town on a small rise just off the main road to Figueres, and 5 kilometres inland from Empuriabrava.

Surrounded on all sides by

"tourist towns", it is as though tourism had never been heard of in Castelló d'Empúries. A look at the 14th-century **Gothic church** with its remarkable porch and statues of the 12 apostles is enough to suggest that this was a town of some importance. It was the capital of the whole neighbourhood and seat of the Counts of Ampurias. The really magnificent church, its vast forecourt, the old cobbled streets, the *Llotja* (old Stock Exchange) and the whole feel of the town remind one of its former opulence. It's all a delightful contrast to the modern coastal villages and developments.

According to records, PERALADA (8 kilometres further inland) was founded in the 9th century and its castle built in the 16th century; and, as things look today, very little has changed since then. The castle was the home of the Counts of Perelada for 400 years, but it serves quite a different purpose today: it has been converted into a casino, one of several in the area.

Another claim to fame: Ramón Muntaner, the 13th-century chronicler and war correspondent who covered the military exploits of the Catalans at the peak of their power, came from Peralada.

But in spite of all this, it is something else that draws flocks to Peralada. If it seems to you that people are reeling strangely, there's an easy explanation: Peralada is famed for its outstanding sparkling

Traffic ban in Roses's main street is a boon to shoppers and strollers.

Castles in Spain

There are 5,000 officially classified castles in the land; some are magnificently preserved or restored (as the fairy-tale Alcázar at Segovia), while others are unidentifiable piles of rubble. During the Reconquest, 10,000 castles, fortified monasteries and farmhouses dotted the landscape as Spaniards poured their energies into the 700-year-long struggle to push back the Moors. So many were there in central Spain that the region to this day is known as *Castilla* (land of castles) and its inhabitants as *Castellanos* (castle-keepers).

Many Spanish castles are privately owned. If you'd like one yourself, write to Asociación Española de Amigos de los Castillos, located at Calle de Bárbara de Braganza, 8, Madrid. They may know of one for sale. Not so long ago castles sold for as little as $4,000. The only trouble is that the repairs might run to as much as $100,000!

white wine, called locally *champán*. The invitation to visit the cellar to sample the sparkling cool wine can go to your head. Otherwise, have a taste of the refreshing drink at the big café near the entrance to the village.

LA JONQUERA is Spain's busiest and best known frontier town, although it lies 6 kilometres from the actual border and is bypassed by the main road. It carries on its own happy existence and ignores the million cars passing in each direction annually in Northern Europe's Iberian summer migration. It has some pleasant houses and a 15th-century church. Nearby **Requesens Castle,** 12 kilometres up a bumpy road through Cantallops, was La Jonquera's frontier sentinel.

Figueres

Figueres, 18 kilometres from Roses, is Girona Province's second largest town. So many visitors stop here for a last shopping spree before continuing up to La Jonquera, the frontier, that the centre of the town gives an impression of being one gigantic market. Austere Sant Ferran Castle, sitting squarely on the hill behind, is not open to the public. Begun in 1743, this military monolith has a girth of over 1 mile, and room enough for 10,000 men and 5,000 horses.

If Figueres has few pretentions to beauty, there is a great deal of character in the maze of back streets off the central *Rambles* (promenade), where something is always going on—*sardana,* exhibitions, or simply the hubbub and excitement in the packed cafés.

But it also has more serious claims to pride. First among them is Salvador Dalí, for the artist was born here, and since 1973 the town's main artistic attraction has been the amazing **Teatre-Museu Dalí.**

Within the maze of streets of the town centre, in the middle of a bare, red-tiled square and beside the very staid Church of Sant Pere, you'll come upon a tortured tree trunk draped in a sheet and topped by some stones and a golden egg. Behind is the imposing façade of the building—a real theatre in the heyday of the town—and you realize you have arrived.

Everybody seems to have an opinion on Dalí, who on his own authority is The World's Greatest Painter. Make up your own mind on the question as you tour this theatre-museum. Circus-ring ushers stand round as part of the décor in this extravagant monument Dalí created to his own ego. Beneath a great cupola ceiling, huge feet appear to be descending on the unwary visitor. In the Mae West Room, a deforming mir-

Modified Cadillac: showpiece in Figueres's Salvador Dalí Museum.

Fishermen at Sant Pere Pescador— Costa Brava's inland fishing port.

ror slung beneath the belly of a stuffed camel dissolves the view of a roomful of furniture into a seemingly three-dimensional portrait of the actress. A Cadillac parked in the patio has a large stone on its roof and a gilt-breasted amazon aforefront. In the curious setting of the theatre, the whole range of Dalí's creation—from the most "conventionally surrealist" to the wildest of his fantasies—can be seen, touched or activated, while all around, animated discussions are heard, punctuated by cries of hilarity—or admiration.

With the same ticket, you can visit the spick-and-span **Museu de l'Empordà** (Empordà Museum) on the Rambles, dedicated to the history of the region and in quite another vein from the last museum. It takes us from Greek and Roman objects to the present day via pottery, woodcarvings, portraits of local notables, landscape paintings and folk art. Picasso, Miró (who dedicated a work to the museum) and (predictably) Dalí are represented.

Just opposite the museum on the central square, framed by the Rambles, stands a statue of Narciso Monturiol (1819–85), who was the local hero (until eclipsed by Dalí). His invention, the wooden submarine, *Ictíneo,* operated manually by a crew of six, slid into Barcelona harbour in mid-summer 1861—a pioneering triumph of the era. The event went unnoticed by the outside world.

The Coast from Roses to Palamós

Sant Pere Pescador is an oddity for the Costa Brava: a fishing village with fishing boats but without sea. It lies on the banks of the River Fluvià, some 3 kilometres from the sea itself—all of which gives an incongruous if delightfully different air to this working fishing community set in an area which is mostly devoted to agriculture.

The safe inland position that protected Sant Pere in the old days has disqualified it for entry into the 20th-century tourist stakes, but allowed it to preserve its real soul. While here, you may wish to make the journey to SANT MIQUEL DE FLUVIÀ, with its remarkable 11th-century Romanesque church.

L'ESCALA, a few miles down the coast at the southern end of the Gulf of Roses, is deservedly an up-and-coming resort. A simple, typical fishing town until recently, its steep and animated streets lead down to a pretty harbour rimmed with waterfront bars and restaurants. The tourists share the beach space with boats, beside which fishermen sit mending their nets. A broad coastal road spans the whole town, but the usual local parking problems persist. Favourite swimming beaches are RIELLS and MONTGÓ, several kilometres to the south.

L'Escala (meaning the stopping place) was a halt on Hannibal's route north. The area is full of historical landmarks, and bathers who appreciate history will surely take a dip below SANT MARTÍ D'EMPÚRIES, with its long, uncluttered, sandy beach. Here, just north of L'Escala, sprawls the most remarkable archaeological site on the Costa Brava—the **ruins of Empúries** (Ampurias), right beside the beach and with some last vestiges in the sea itself.

In the 6th century B.C., Sant Martí d'Empúries was a small island. Greek settlers built a port on the island that came to be known as Palaeopolis (the old city). Not long afterwards, they constructed another port, later called Neapolis (the new city), on the mainland a few hundred yards away. When the Romans came, they extended the whole complex and called it Emporion (after the Greek word for trading post).

The Roman city thrived until the 5th century when Visigothic invasions from the north brought about a rapid decline. By the time the Moors were sweeping through Spain, it stood in ruins, and the sand and silt of centuries had linked Sant Martí to the mainland.

When L'Escala began to expand in the 1600s, the former splendour of Empúries was only a legend of old, passed down from generation to generation—and a quarry from which the people of L'Escala could take stone to build their houses. Great blocks of masonry left for destinations as far afield as Roses and Perpignan in France.

Then, in 1908, excavations unearthed the boundaries of the 700-by-500-yard ancient settlement of Empúries and revealed the long-buried treasures of the town. The most sensational find was a larger-than-life statue of Asclepius (the Greek god of medicine), sculpted in marble from an Athenian quarry. The original has been moved to the Barcelona Archaeological Museum, but a copy stands in its place in the ruined temple dedicated to the god. Another copy is in the museum right on the site, which exhibits most of the finds made here.

Wander through the ancient cities of two civilizations; it is a vivid experience. You pass water storage cisterns, ground plans of two patrician villas, huge defence walls, ruined temples, the old market-places, the baths and houses. You'll be able to imagine the place alive with people going about their everyday occupations; you'll marvel at the achievements of their civilization.

Then look in at the museum with its ceramics, jewels, household items, weapons, multicoloured mosaics and statues rescued from centuries of oblivion. Outside the museum, still intact on the mosaic floor, is a touching inscription in Greek that has survived the ravages of time and invasion: "Sweet Dreams".

Ruins of Empúries bear mute witness to a history of two civilizations.

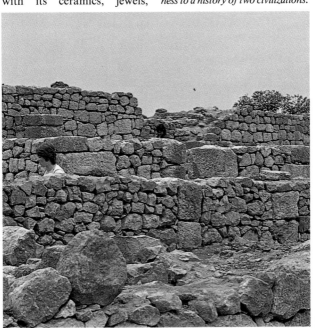

L'Estartit

L'Estartit, at the top of the long Bay of Pals, was only a huddle of modest fishermen's houses at the foot of the striking Roca Maura until the tourist boom of the 1960s transformed it overnight into a thriving holiday spot and a major yachting centre. The broad sandy beach is excellent for children, but beware of the occasional day when waves can be tall. Attractions include launch excursions to coastal destinations inaccessible by land and to the ILLES MEDES whose jagged profile looms offshore.

The largest island is Meda Gran; you won't find buried treasures here, but at least after a visit to the island, you can claim to have explored a genuine pirates' lair, for Normans, Algerians and Turks all used the islands as a base from which to terrorize the coast. In the 15th century, monks established a fortified monastery there, and during the Peninsular War, the British occupied the territory until driven out by French shore batteries in L'Estartit. Since 1890, except for the lighthouse, the islands have been uninhabited—to the delight of botanists, who can find over 150 identified species of plants.

Five kilometres inland from L'Estartit lies TORROELLA DE MONTGRÍ, a favourite shopping centre for visitors up and down the coast. Its colourful market sells the pick of local Mediterranean fruit and seafood and some imaginative items from wickerwork artisans of the area.

In the 13th century Torroella was a port, but during the last 700 years, the River Ter has poured so much silt into the area that the town now lies totally inland. On a barren hill behind stands the gaunt unfinished Montgrí Castle, started on the orders of Jaime II in the 13th century. At that time,

Torroella was famous for more than its weavers; it was a renowned cultural and social centre as well. But a 14th-century epidemic decimated the population, and by the 1600s a combination of wars and pirate raids had wrecked the town. The castle serves as a powerful reminder of a time when Torroella was one of the favourite royal hunting retreats.

Left: *Picking from among the many Mediterranean vegetables is a joy.*
Below: *The broad and sandy beaches typify L'Estartit, a yachting centre.*

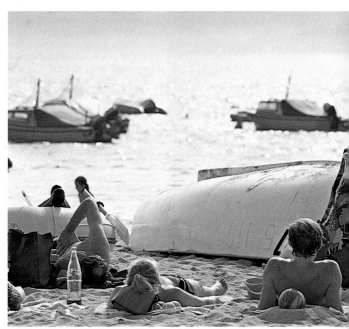

Begur

The next point of importance down the coast is Begur. In spite of Begur's location, 4 kilometres inland, the role of the sea can always be felt in the town. Begur plays "capital" to five small, charming and popular beach resorts strung along the rugged coastline, all quite different in character. First to come, and just out of sight of the long sandy beach of Pals, is

SA RIERA, where fishermen's houses mingle with more modern constructions in a successful blend. Then follow AIGUA-FREDA, SA TUNA, FORNELLS and AIGUABLAVA with its mysterious rock formations.

Villas huddle among the trees at Begur, many belonging to wealthy families from Barcelona, others built by *indianos,* those who returned rich from the Latin-American colonies. These elegant, small mansions, with wrought-iron window grills, arcaded balconies and plain, stark colours on the walls, are surrounded by palm-trees redolent of the tropics. Some of these *indianos* also built similarly attractive summer houses on the beach of Sa Tuna.

The massive ruined castle above Begur stands on the site of an earlier fortress which withstood countless attacks by Norman and Scandinavian raiders and a motley bunch of Mediterranean pirates. From its ruins you have a magnificent view over the coast and the hinterland.

At Aiguablava, a state-run inn of the national *parador* chain (see below) perches high

Idyllic coves abound in Begur area.

above a sheltered cove, its foundations built into the rock.

From here, take a boat to the COVA D'EN GISPERT, a cave that cuts 900 feet into the cliff. It may take a bit of stiff negotiation with the local fishermen, but the 1–2-hour cruise is well worth-while. And if you don't find Aiguablava's water particularly refreshing, try the nearby Cove of Aigua Xelida ("freezing water"); the difference is astounding.

Spain's Parador Chain

There are nearly one hundred *paradores* (state-run tourist inns) in Spain's national *parador* chain. They are dotted strategically around the country so that a traveller is never more than a day's drive away from one.

Twenty hotels have been installed in converted castles or palaces; a further ten in other buildings of outstanding historical and architectural interest. And apart from elegant surroundings and menus featuring typical regional dishes, *paradores* offer service and facilities unheard of elsewhere in Europe at the price. The organization employs nearly one staff member per guest (maximum stay: 10 days).

Paradores are not in competition with commercial hotels, and in fact they lose money. Their job is to promote Spain and help open up little-frequented but worthy tourist areas.

The most popular inns are often fully booked two months in advance, so it is advisable to reserve early. On the Costa Brava, there is a very luxurious *parador* at Aiguablava; elsewhere in Catalonia they are located at Vic, Cardona (near a unique salt mountain), Balaguer, Tortosa and Vall d'Arán.

Inland from Begur

Within easy reach of Begur are a series of points of interest in the heart of the Catalonian countryside.

Apart from the occasional tractor and roadside advertisement, PALS (5 kilometres from Begur), in common with a number of other villages in this area, seems barely changed since its origins in the 10th century. Cars can go only as far as the old church; the rest must be visited on foot. The harmonious colour of the stone, the long, walled precincts, the tower *(Torre de les Hores)* crowning the hill, the narrow streets and attractive houses go to make up a complete living museum.

The charming inland village of Pals, dating from the 10th century, is dominated by Torre de les Hores.

Along with parts of Valencia, further south, the Pals region is one of Spain's rice-growing areas, though this activity is losing its impetus here as time goes by and tourism takes over the key role. Each June, however, the farmers work 12 hours a day up to their knees in the muddy paddies sowing the new crop.

Pals boasts its own beach, PLATJA DE PALS, 6 kilometres

away. Though the tall radio transmitters in the background scarcely contribute to creating a holiday atmosphere, the long stretch of perfect sand —so hot at times it's hard to walk on barefoot—and a golf course spreading out among the pine trees that grow in profusion explain the beach's popularity.

Peratallada nestles in the fertile Empordà plain, unchanging and unchanged for generations. Once heavily fortified, remnants of its defensive walls still stand, totally integrated into a beautiful stone town of a harmonious grey-yellow hue. Poplars and flowers abound to add touches of colour and life. Old dogs bask in the leaden sun; chickens, flapping their wings hysterically, flutter across beaten-earth tracks (none of the roads are paved); walls, churches, towers, arcades and galleries fit in together in this timeless, most unselfconscious complex. One rather run-down shop and a lonely restaurant bravely represent commercial activity. The names of former owners appear engraved on the lintels of various old houses.

Thirty years ago, ULLASTRET (10 kilometres from Torroella) was an unknown hamlet, charming but unremarkable in the area. Today, the name is familiar to scholars throughout Catalonia and far beyond, for, in 1946, archaeologists excavating the hill of Sant Andreu unearthed an entire 4th–5th century B.C. **Iberian city.** Lengthy walls have been excavated, grain silos and subterranean water tanks survive, and the whole site has been neatly labeled with plans and numerous explanations. The museum, set amid gardens with benches and even a picnic area, exhibits objects found during the dig. Greek vases stand beside skulls with rusty swords still protruding from them. Arms, instruments, implements, pottery and everyday objects all constitute a small but instructive museum.

Palafrugell

TAMARIU, LLAFRANC and CALELLA (near Cap Roig Botanical Gardens, with the rocky ILLES FORMIGUES offshore) are three deservedly popular and secluded resorts fanning out from inland Palafrugell; each is built on steep hills enclosing picturesque small bays. Pine trees descend right down to sea level, adding their fragrance to the smell of the sea. **39**

Palafrugell, an important market town for the surrounding farming communities, is also a favourite shopping spot for holiday-makers. Unlike Begur, an inland sea-town, Palafrugell, in spite of its tentacular hold on its resorts, turns its back on the sea to look inland. Its prosperity stems from both a cosmopolitan tourist trade and the cork industry, for it stands on the edge of La Selva, one of the great cork-producing areas of Spain. If, at some point, you feel the need for solitude, you can be alone here with scarcely a sign of human presence, while the coast is no more than 15 kilometres away.

Visit the 15th-century Gothic **Església de Sant Martí** (Church of St. Martin), restored after Civil War damage. Take a break from shopping to sample a *vino negro* ("black wine") in one of the town's bars. Red wine is called *tinto* elsewhere in Spain, but the dark-red, strong Empordà type, with up to 17 per cent alcohol content, deserves its name.

At LA BISBAL (13 kilometres from Palafrugell) further shopping possibilities await a visitor, especially in the way of local pottery—vivid, though not garish. And visit the 13th-century fortified **Palacio de los Obispos** (Palace of the Bishops), now in a poor state of repair. From 844 to 1446, the town was ruled by the Church after it was given to the Bishop of Girona by the Frankish king, Charles the Bald.

Round La Bisbal lie many other charming villages, such as CRUÏLLES, MADREMANYA and SANT MARTÍ VELL perfect in their way, totally closed to the industrial world, doomed to decline as their young are irresistibly drawn to the cities.

Palamós

Back now to the coast, with one of the star resorts of the Costa Brava. Palamós's affluence has always been linked with its **port**. In 1299, the Catalonian fleet set out from here to conquer Sicily; the valiant expedition that beat the Turks at Lepanto assembled at Palamós where, on a number of occasions, the French navy also landed its invading forces. Today it harbours the town's sizeable fishing fleet. Alongside, a marina for 500 pleasure and sports-craft symbolizes the community's entry into the tourist industry.

Palamós's fleet casts off at dawn and returns in the late afternoon. The catch, an eye-opening selection of Mediterranean sea-life, provides the ingredients for such delicious Catalan dishes as *suquet de peix*. Watch it being auctioned at 5 o'clock in *La Llotja,* the auction-room. Here is the chance to spend half an hour in the fisherman's world, amongst sea-going boats, wives mending mounds of nets and brawny, rough-talking sea-dogs. No hope of under-

standing much of what the auctioneer is saying. He mumbles at the rate of 500 words a minute—in Catalan.

Also visit the 15th-century **Church of Santa Maria del Mar** (St. Mary of the Sea), which still dominates the skyline. During the Spanish Civil War,

Enter the universe of the fisherman at 5 p.m. in Palamós, as the catch of the day is auctioned off briskly.

Palamós was bombed but the church came out unscathed. Damage to the town was repaired by the government's Devastated Regions Service, an organization Palamós could have done with in 1543 when it was sacked by the feared pirate Barbarossa (Red Beard), who meted out the

same treatment to Cadaqués. And don't miss the town's museum, **Cau de la Costa Brava,** with exhibits recalling the former thriving cork industry. You'll be overwhelmed by the nuances and qualities there can be of a simple bottle-stopper! Also excellent collections of local Iberian, Greek and Roman ceramics, and seashells and coins (Palamós minted its own in the 15th century).

Smooth beach and calm sea combine agreeably for bathers and boaters.

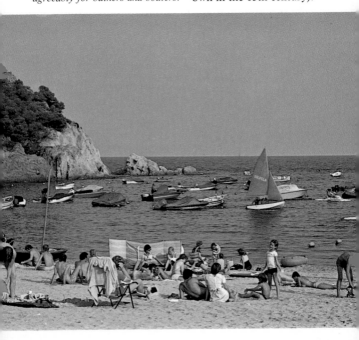

The Southern Stretch

The broad sweep of clean, white beach made Palamós, neighbouring SANT ANTONI DE CALONGE and LA PLATJA D'ARO obvious targets for developers. Tourism in fact created La Platja d'Aro. It is now a pleasant, bustling resort, well planned if one can ignore the towering skyscrapers right on the beach. Some 25 years ago, there existed only the broad, uninterrupted expanse of beach—the rest was open countryside.

S'Agaró and Sant Feliu de Guíxols

Visitors have only words of praise for what they find at S'Agaró (3 kilometres beyond La Platja d'Aro), small, exclusive and elegant—no untidy *urbanizaciones* or haphazard planning here.

The town, begun from scratch in 1923, was the brainchild of a Girona businessman, José Ensesa, who set out to transform a few empty acres into a residential town without ugly urban sprawl. He set up iron-clad contracts with his clients to guarantee the architectural integrity of the project and took advantage of the rocky cliffs (for we have again left behind the long, sandy stretches). All the luxurious houses cling to seaside cliffs or peer discreetly through deep pine-tree cover. There are parks, public and private gardens, lookout points, rotundas and the magnificent 2½-mile-long **Camí de Ronda,** a promenade that follows the contour of the coast. Steps lead down to SA CONCA beach on one side of the town, while SANT POL beach on the other is the only place on the Costa Brava where there is a small charge to go onto the sand and make use of the bathing huts.

In keeping with this aura of exclusivity, S'Agaró boasts one of Spain's most famous hotels, the Hostal de La Gavina, where you will have no trouble whatsoever spending a small fortune for an—admittedly—unforgettable stay, perhaps in the Louis XV suite with marble bathroom and genuine period furniture, or, more modestly, in a double room where your slightest wish is a command.

According to tradition, the Iberian King Brigo, searching for an easily defensible yet beautiful bay, fell for the site of Sant Feliu de Guíxols and had a castle built there, captured centuries later by **43** the Moors. Later still, Charlemagne converted it into a Benedictine monastery which still exists, though changed and restored over the years. Today, remnants of the original survive amidst some Gothic architecture, such as the **Porta Ferrada,** an elegant, arcaded 11th-century gallery, restored in 1931, and the **Torre del Fum** (Smoke Signal Tower) where fires were lit to warn of pirate attack. The museum, close by, in its modest way, confirms the breadth of the town's history.

Sant Feliu, the self-dubbed "Queen of the Costa Brava", lies 3 kilometres south of S'Agaró and shares the beach (the non-exclusive part) with it. Bright and pleasant, with a large resident population, Sant Feliu has just about everything that can be expected of a Costa Brava holiday. This long-established resort exudes a stylish Riviera-like charm and has avoided the look of a boom town. At the same time, it provides all the necessary amenities—good shops and restaurants, tours and excursions by land or sea, a yacht marina, golf club, tennis courts, riding stables, nightclubs and a bullring. It has a short but active promenade, its Rambles, and an exceptionally broad and beautiful marine boulevard. The elegant old buildings lining this leafy **Passeig de Mar** were designed as casinos. The beach in front is broad, sandy and open, with the possibility of trips up to more deserted coves and crags, difficult of access except by boat.

For the best view of the town and typical coastal scenery it is worth taking a short walk to the **Ermita de Sant Elm** (Hermitage of St. Elm). From here, the town looks neat and prosperous (its original wealth came essentially from the cork industry); turn to face the south and the rugged coast stretches away towards Tossa, 22 kilometres beyond. The churning sea below surges around the rocks, sucking the waters into crannies and spewing them out furiously. A plaque cut into the rock mentions that on this spot, Ferrán Agulló conceived the idea of baptizing the coast Costa Brava ("wild coast").

Night-time activity now concentrates on bars, clubs and discotheques, and on the *Passeig* itself, where, on warm nights, families and courting couples stroll and chat in the inimitable Iberian babble of excitement and communication. Once a week in the summer (check at the Tourist Office in the Town Hall), the *sardana* is danced on the *Passeig* or in front of the Town Hall. If you feel the urge, join in with a fringe group (see p. 81). But don't be upset if you find yourself edged out for upsetting the tempo of the entire circle.

Inland from Sant Feliu

On a hilltop 6 kilometres from Sant Feliu is Pedralta, Iberia's biggest balancing rock. One huge stone atop another of the same caliber can be levered and rocked without it toppling. To get there, leave Sant Feliu on the Girona road, and at the last row of houses in the town, take the small turning to the left. But if you drive, don't be too hard on your car's suspension, as the track becomes progressively more bumpy and full of potholes.

CALDES DE MALAVELLA (23 kilometres inland from Sant Feliu) can claim no prominent sons and was never the scene of a famous battle; yet it has enjoyed a widespread reputation for 2,000 years. *Calda* means a hot mineral water spring, and the spas at Caldes have been visited since Roman times by sufferers from gastric **45** and rheumatic complaints. In 1883, the water was declared "of public utility" and now it is bottled commercially. But you can drink it as it emerges from the ground— only beware: it's so hot it almost scorches your mouth. It dribbles pitifully from a small fountain behind the Roman remains. You'll notice a few bottles lying beside the rather insignificant fountain waiting to be picked up. Another, and somewhat more grandiose, fountain at the entrance to the town gushes forth torrents when operated manually.

Driving up the N11 near SILS, at kilometre 706, you will find the **Colecció d'Automòbils de Salvador Claret** (the Salvador Claret Vintage Car Museum). Señor Claret started his collection in the 1920s and acquired a display of 80 antique cars, each reconditioned by him personally and each in perfect working order. The oldest is an 1883 single-cylinder, coal-burning Merry Weather.

Tossa de Mar

From Sant Feliu to Tossa (a distance of 22 kilometres), the road twists and turns, following the sinuous course of the coast. Few of the hidden creeks are easily accessible, but the views are magnificent. Keep an eye on the road.

Of all the big resorts on the Costa Brava, Tossa de Mar can claim to be one of the most attractive.

Twenty years before Spain's tourist boom got under way, Tossa was a hideaway for artists in search of cheap living, beautiful surroundings and mild weather. Things have not greatly changed: then, as now, Spain was relatively cheap and the Mediterranean summer meant dazzling sunrise and endless dusk. The white village with a touch of the South and the profile of the old fortified city standing out against the southern skyline, spelled paradise for painters and writers sick of the grit and grime of city life.

No Tossa School as such emerged, but fine work was produced in this fishing village clustered harmoniously round Tossa Bay. Roads of the old town are named after the main Catalan artists such as the Plaça J. Villalonga, and examples of their work hang today in the museum built right into the walls of Vila Vella (the old fortified city)—gifts from those artists who at one time or another called Tossa their home.

The museum also displays

relics of Tossa's Roman era, when it was known as Turissa. At the back of the town, on its outskirts, you can see an excavated Roman villa, complete with mosaics, its own swimming pool and a sophisticated heating system. Children, under careful surveillance, excavate further with all the enthusiasm of gold-diggers.

The great 12th-century walls of **Vila Vella** (3 feet thick in places and some 23 feet high) once held back savage marauders. By the 17th century, the town had started to outgrow its walls; a new church was consecrated in 1776 just in front of the large beach round the bay, and around it sprang up the modern town. Delightful, fresh

Tossa's ramparts form backdrop for bathers as new houses gleam in sun.

and inviting though this new town is, visitors tend to head to Vila Vella to inspect its crumbling archways, rough cobbled streets with a profusion of flowers and a galaxy of galleries, bars and restaurants in ancient houses built of the same stone as the ramparts. Remains of medieval wall house tool sheds and dog kennels.

The fortified wall encircles the hill on which the old town lies; one tower (Torre Major) and part of the wall that gave onto the sea were demolished to make way for the lighthouse, but three towers remain, and a magnificent view can be had of "wild" coastal scenery.

There is something of an air of conspiracy, of smuggling and piracy about the minute **Es Codolar Cove,** tucked away at the back of Vila Vella and enclosed on either side by abrupt hillsides. In fact, however, this cove has for centuries provided safe anchorage for Tossa's fishermen and was their original home. Their boats are pulled high up the slope of the beach almost to the foot of the last tower. The slowly diminishing number of fishermen share the cove with tourists who swim there during the day, sometimes turning

up early in the morning to watch the catch brought home.

The rocky coast between here and Blanes, 20 kilometres further down the coast, is much appreciated by skindivers.

Only a narrow riverbed (today a parking place) separates modern Tossa from its main beach. Down on the sand, booths sell excursion tickets for boats bobbing in the shallows. Even when dusk approaches, "action" scarcely moves from the water's edge. Beachside restaurants spring to life as hundreds of hungry holiday-makers pack outdoor tables and unhurriedly sip aperitifs as they wait to eat at the Spanish hour—when the heat of the day has abated. And, just before darkness falls, arc lamps silently explode into life, throwing into relief the venerable walls of Vila Vella against an ink-blue sky.

Lloret de Mar

There could scarcely be a bigger contrast to Tossa than Lloret de Mar: the one town is slow-moving, leisurely; the other, brash, full of life, noise, movement.

Lloret is unabashedly, enthusiastically a tourist town—

with a Spanish coloration. It hasn't the beauty of Tossa, but, for animated nightlife, for "holiday life" in community, there is no town on the Costa Brava like Lloret. More than 200 hotels, one casino, and shops, discos, clubs and restaurants by the thousand are jumbled behind the palm-shaded **Passeig Verdaguer.** This boulevard, perhaps the most elegant seafront promenade on the entire Costa Brava, provides a fine background for the immense, broad sandy beach sweeping around Lloret Bay.

On a rocky promontory at one end of the bay stands a mighty, turreted castle whose medieval outline is an obvious favourite with photographers. But on closer inspection, if you feel something amiss, something a bit too perfect, you would be right: the castle (a classic postcard view) is Lloret's very own folly, built this century by a Barcelona businessman who had the bank-balance to match his dreams.

The maze of streets leading into the Passeig Verdaguer form the heart of a cosmopolitan shopping centre—don't even attempt to enter by car. To get the feel of Lloret's multinational character, just take a

stroll round in early evening. Here, amid a wild contrast of exotic aromas and multilingual neon signs, German beer-halls compete with English tea-rooms and the fish-and-chips shops; here, smørgåsbord, spaghetti, sauerkraut, sau-

Barcelona businessman built castle "guarding" beach at Lloret de Mar.

sages, mash and other "imported" dishes are in heavy demand by sun-tanned hordes, ravenous after their daily beach stints. Search hard enough amongst the crowded streets and culinary hotch- **49** potch and you'll even find Catalan and Castilian specialities—in a restaurant most likely owned by a Finn or an Englishman.

Lloret today has no industry but tourism, yet its history and traditions go back centuries. Probably founded by the Iberians, it was certainly colonized by the Romans. In the Middle Ages, it boasted a serious castle, and, in the 13th century, Italian sailors formed a colony here.

The ship-building industry has disappeared now, and the fishing fleet has dwindled to a handful of boats beached in La Caleta Cove. Tourism has swept all before it: fishermen have become shop-owners and bartenders; farmers, property magnates; brick-layers, contractors and promotors. One fisherman whose great-great-grandfather died in South American swamps searching for gold found *his* gold-mine without leaving home. His family's sea-side shanty became valuable overnight and is now the site of a ten-storey, three-star hotel.

A few calm islets held out, however, against the invasion. One or two dour fishermen tend their nets stoically; Tuesday remains market-day; on Sunday, black-shrouded women hurry arm in arm past bikini-clad visitors to attend mass at **Sant Romà,** Lloret's 16th-century church with its multi-coloured tiles standing out like a sore thumb. And almost any balmy evening, groups of villagers may gather to dance the *sardana* beneath the palms of Passeig Verdaguer, which maintains its dignified old-world charm. The best way to take in Lloret's possibilities is to stand and admire the graceful curve of the lovely bay from here.

Lloret's most popular annual fiesta, enjoyed equally by townspeople and tourists, is held in honour of St. Christine, an Italian martyr killed by arrows. Her corpse was hurled into the sea with a stone attached and found still intact by Lloret fishermen months later. A **hermitage** was built in St. Christine's honour on the pine-covered bluff above the beach where her body was found. The delightful beach, with its single hotel and cultivated fields all round, was named after her and she was also made Lloret's Protector of Fishermen.

Now, each year, on the morning of July 24th, decorated boats are launched from Lloret to sail the nearly 2 miles to **Santa Cristina Cove.** Then, boatmen and ex-boatmen, returning to their original profession for the day, and hundreds of lazier villagers who have travelled by road, climb to the hermitage to pay homage to the saint—and celebrate afterwards in the hearty Catalan way.

Costa Brava lures the adventurous.

Blanes

For Blanes, tourism is just a rich bonus for an already stable economy. Its deep-sea fishing fleet remains in action, farmers continue to till the surrounding land, and a booming nylon factory employs 4,000 workers. Blanes's long history has left noteworthy ruins and its beaches are as fine as any on the Catalonian coast. A long maritime promenade, with playground and carpark, faces a beach with two minute islands which mark the official limit of the Costa Brava.

Hints of Blanes's past wealth can be seen on the seafront: some of the aristocratic houses, mingling in with the modern blocks, were built by *indianos* back from Latin America.

Behind the seafront, the town has kept its character of a fishing town (though this industry has become secondary) with a maze of narrow backstreets.

The wild beauty of the cliffs along its northern shoreline has attracted a large number of nature-lovers to make their home in Blanes. One of the first was Carlos Faust, born in Germany in 1874, who emigrated to Spain in his youth. After making his fortune in Barcelona, he came to Blanes

These rugged fishermen, busily at work on their trawler, perpetuate the sea-going tradition in Blanes.

and bought a large plot of land north of the town overlooking the Mediterranean. There, in 1928, he planted a garden, **Marimurtra** (sea and myrtle), which gained fame throughout the botanical world. He had arranged for the gardens to pass to a trust after his death in 1952, and now Marimurtra is tended by botanists and a team of nine gardeners who look after more than 3,000 different species of trees, shrubs and flowers. From the rotunda on a rocky promontory at the edge of the gardens, you see a Capuchin monastery plus some breathtaking seascapes. Open to the public, Marimurtra is a major attraction; the serene beauty and the dazzling colours of the flowers make a welcome change from the beach.

On the quay in Blanes, two glimpses of the world of the deep: first, at the **aquarium,** with its living panorama of Mediterranean sea life; then, at the daily fish auction (held nearby), with more of the same... but ready for filleting.

In town, look in on the **Parish Church of Santa Maria** (St. Mary's). Built in the 14th century, it was restored after serious damage in the Civil War, though the outside has retained all its charm. Inside, the vault keystones carry the coats-of-arms of the Cabrera family, who owned whole tracts of countryside throughout Catalonia. Their palace once was linked to the church. Today a few bits of rubble testify to the building's existence; also, some 300 yards beyond, half hidden down one of the main streets, is a 15th-century Gothic fountain which served the household.

Blanes is the southernmost coastal town in the Province of Girona; we have come to the end of the Costa Brava. The coastline changes character, losing its "wild" look to

become flat, with long sandy beaches. South of Blanes begins the Costa del Maresme*. Inland from Blanes and on the border with Barcelona Province stands the intriguing 11th-century walled village of HOSTALRIC.

The renowned Marimurtra Gardens in Blanes, laid out in 1928, attract both the botanist and the tourist.

* See the Berlitz BARCELONA AND COSTA DORADA Travel Guide.

Girona—Capital of the Costa Brava

Bridges and staircases—this is the image you are likely to take back with you of Girona (Gerona in Castilian). You'll be surprised by the fascination of this small city. Turn almost any corner in old Girona and you'll come upon some surprising monument, a ometres from Sant Feliu de Guíxols, the closest resort, and less than 80 from Portbou, the furthest. A trip to this compact town with a long history is an ideal opportunity to sample Spanish city life and at the same time a chance to shop at competitive prices. From anywhere on the Costa Brava, the journey and some leisurely sightseeing can be fitted comfortably into one day.

GIRONA OLD CITY

revelation or a delight. Stairways worn smooth by centuries of footsteps lead under arches invaded by weeds. Narrow alleys, cobbled tracks between crumbling walls, guide you through a medieval panorama.

Capital of the province and, by extension, of the Costa Brava, Girona lies just 35 kilometres from Sant Feliu de

Girona was founded several centuries B.C. at the confluence of the rivers Ter and Onyar (Oñar in Castilian). Ten bridges and one square cross the Onyar as it cuts through the town. Although the river normally runs 10 feet below tenements and shops whose windows hang out romantically over the waters, it has, more prosaically, been a source of misery since time immemorial to the Gironese; the river quite regularly overflows—eight or ten times a century since records began in the 13th century. One bar, so close to the river as to be uninsurable, has wall marks recording the heights of no less than six floods, one as recently as 1970.

The River Onyar divides the city neatly in two, a geographical convenience helping visitors find their bearings. In front is the old quarter, called **Barri de la Catedral,** containing all that is of interest to the visitor, and behind, Barri del Mercadal, the far bigger commercial and residential section.

The most typical street of the old quarter is the steep **Carrer de la Força,** once the heart of the old Jewish quarter. Art galleries, antique shops, printing shops and stalls specializing in precious books blend discreetly with the stern Gothic architecture of its ancient buildings. At No. 13 is the **Museu de la Ciutat** (Museum of City History), with exhibits recalling notable Gironese feats of arms and an entire room devoted to manuscripts of typical Gironese *sardana* music.

Strolling up the Carrer de la Força, you feel that no real upheaval has changed life since the Middle Ages—except for the plague of cars barely able to turn in the tight one-way streets. Don't even attempt to drive up to the cathedral.

Carrer de la Força runs directly to the Plaça Catedral. A fine monumental Baroque stairway of 90 steps leads up to the cathedral's Door of the Apostles, a magnificent entrance so badly damaged during the Civil War that only two of the 12 apostles' statues are originals. The **cathedral** dates from the 11th century, but was subsequently enlarged during the 14th and 15th. The result is a nave of impressive proportions, flanked all round by 30 side chapels. If light and your eyes permit, try to scrutinize the vault keystones of these chapels. Each is a masterpiece in itself.

Through huge stained-glass windows, the muted light filters onto the gilded altarpieces of the chapels and illuminates the majestic interior, usually empty of chairs; rarely does a cathedral present such an awesome sight. The carved, alabaster high altar has served the church since its consecration day in 1038. In the adjoining **55** chapter-house, the **cathedral treasure** includes two important items: in a room to itself, a 12th-century tapestry in charming low-key colours telling the story of the Creation, and the *Book of the Apocalypse,* an illuminated manuscript of texts and commentaries compiled by a certain Friar Beato in the Asturian Monastery of Liébana in A.D. 975. There are also superb medieval gold and silver plates, magnificent medieval Catalonian wooden sculptures and paintings, and some lovely Moorish chests.

In a region where beautiful cloisters are relatively abundant, Girona's **cloister** is exceptional; the anecdotal Old Testament sculpture will delight you. Two angels sit chatting on a wall. A sheepish, bearded Adam has a bite from an apple resembling a hand grenade. In front of the restful cloister, the 12th-century Romanesque bell tower, called "Charlemagne's Tower", rises imposingly.

Squatting at the cathedral's feet, though a fairly massive work itself, is the **Església Sant Fèlix** (St. Felix's Church), thought to stand over catacombs where the 4th-century St. Narcissus was martyred during a secret Mass. The

catacombs were Girona's first Christian burial ground. St. Felix, also martyred, was the 4th-century Bishop of Girona and is now the city's patron saint. The church's foundations were laid in 1313 and the building completed in 1392. The elegant Gothic spire, mimicked by the nearby poplars, remains one of Girona's most delightful and characteristic landmarks, for its top ten feet were lopped off by lightning in 1581 and never replaced. Inside, you'll see Roman (or, in fact, early-Christian) sarcophaguses with beautifully carved scenes of the life of Susanna and Narcissus's own very fine tomb.

Tucked away behind a wall near the cathedral, the so-called **Banys àrabs** (Arab Baths) were built 400 years after the Moors were expelled from Catalonia; they imitate a Moorish style modelled in turn on Roman baths. Visit the graceful octagonal *frigidarium* (cold bath), the *tepidarium* (warm bath) and *caldarium* (steam bath).

Gerona's fairly modest **Museu Arqueològic Provincial** (Archaeological Museum) is a building of exceptional beauty—the former 12th-century Benedictine Monastery of **Sant Pere de Galligans.** Its exhibits include Greek and Roman objects excavated at Empúries (see pp. 31–33), paintings, including works by Tintoretto and Murillo, and a rare 17th-century printing press. Each May, culture bows to horticulture, and the cool, arcaded monastery cloisters are host to the province's best attended flower display. Note just beside the museum the very delightful Romanesque Church of Sant Nicolau.

Go up some flights of stairs beyond Sant Pere and join the **Passeig Reina Joana,** meandering along the medieval walls which defended Girona (sometimes not too successfully) in no fewer than 34 sieges. Walls, ruined or still standing, battlements, old houses, abandoned or otherwise, appear, disappear, reappear over several hundred yards. Massive towers and buttresses resist, testifying to the moments of glory and decline of a city strategically built to control the plain—and thus the road south—between the Pyrenees and the sea.

In shades of ochre and cream, old Girona's houses crowd the banks of the River Onyar.

The most unusual, profitable and picturesque shopping is to be had in the old quarter. Centuries-old shops with painted wooden fronts remind a visitor that in Girona shopping remains a community affair, not a mad in-and-out rush to grab a few ready-packaged necessities. Here in the casual muddle of Gironese alleys, family businesses flourish. Grocers display tasty, locally produced sausage and cheese, and scoop cereals from open vats or olives galore from great containers. Little old ladies, "embroidery specialists", hand-sew initials onto linen; the owner of a *corsetería,* or corset shop, will happily make garments to fit anyone's particular problem.

The shaded Rambla de la Llibertat, running parallel to the River Onyar, fills the need of every Spanish town for an elegant meeting place. In the mornings, it blazes with colour as flower-sellers bustle amid their dazzling displays.

Regal staircases, bridges, arches form the hallmarks of old Girona.

Late afternoon, friends of all states and ages come together for aperitifs and gossip. With the evening appear the *sardana* dancers and the young who wander endlessly arm-in-arm back and forth along its length, chatting noisily over the general hubbub.

At sunset, people stroll past the Rambles and lean on the railings to stare at the river.

The Road to Andorra

The road to Andorra, after leaving the coast and passing through Girona, begins to rise to the Pyrenees. It follows essentially the same route as the so-called Romanesque Road, which is studded with numerous architectural gems of this period.

While Romanesque art in other Spanish provinces shows distinct Arab influences, in Catalonia, there are more traces of Lombard and Frankish art. The Gironese route links up with the *Route Romane du Roussillon* on the French side of the Pyrenees; Roussillon was part of the Catalonian-Aragonese kingdom until the Treaty of the Pyrenees in 1659, when it was handed over to France.

Banyoles

Banyoles, 18 kilometres from Girona, is a rarity in Spain; a town with a lake. Its origins go back to the Visigothic period and relics of its long history are to be found scattered round the town: a 13th-century church, a monastery dating

A Spanish rarity: Banyoles, a town which boasts a lake of its own.

back to the 9th century and the **Plaça d'Espanya,** bordered all round by an arcade and 15th-century houses. The **Museu Arqueològic** (Archaeological Museum), installed in a carefully restored 15th-century house, boasts Roman and medieval exhibits and the city's historical archives.

The **lake** is a peaceful picnic spot, with cafés purveying food and drink, couples lazily

rowing in search of quiet spots amongst tall trees lining the shore and artists seeking to capture pastel shades on their canvas. Banyoles has also become an important centre for fishing, sailing and water-skiing competitions.

On the opposite side of the lake from Banyoles lies **Porqueres,** a hamlet of two houses, whose small, exquisite 12th-century Romanesque church between the row of trees is a perfect example of harmony between architecture and nature.

Besalú

Besalú captures the spirit of medieval Catalonia at the height of its power in a way no other town does. It may have been founded by the Celts, was certainly an important Roman stronghold, and reached its zenith between the 9th and 12th centuries, when it was the home of the Counts of Besalú.

Monuments still surviving amongst the narrow stone streets include the thousand-year-old **Església de Sant Vicenç** (St. Vincent's Church), which suffered in the Civil War. When reconstruction started, a vase was found beneath the altar containing gold coins and unidentified religious relics. The **Monestir de Sant Pere** (St. Peter's Monastery), founded in 997, and the evocative ruins of the **Església de Santa Maria** (St. Mary's Church), dating from 1055, are located in the upper part of town on a site once occupied by a castle and now private land. Besalú's most famed landmark, admired even by those who drive by the town without stopping, is the arched and fortified **medieval bridge,** recently restored and classified as a national monument. As so often in Spain, a fine massive structure crosses a mere trickle of a stream far below.

Between Besalú and Olot, 20 kilometres away, the village of **Castellfollit de la Roca** perches on a dramatic spur of rock over 300 feet above the River Fluvià. Its church at one end and the rows of houses seem to be suspended over the abyss like the prow of some gigantic stranded ship, while away beyond, the terraced fields climb towards open hills. It is a spectacular sight, particularly at night.

Camprodon

Twisting and turning as it rises from Olot, the road to Camprodon, 30 kilometres north, takes us to another world. The mountain air is brisk and bracing, the shops are overflowing with Pyrenean sausage, cheeses, ham; the people look robust and red-cheeked. At an altitude of over 3,000 feet, and a mere 17 kilometres from the French border, Camprodon is a quite exceptionally pretty mountain village. Have a look before entering the village at the 10th-century **Monastery of Sant Pere.**

The town straggles along the confluence of the rivers Ter and Ritort, forming a perfect *Y*-shape. The focal point is the high-arched 15th-century bridge, inexplicably called **Pont Nou,** or the "new bridge". Excellent fishing and shooting and nearby skiing have made the town a favourite with Gironese, who come on regular weekend pilgrimages here.

But the charm of the village is its houses hanging out over the River Ter as it dashes down from the mountains; for the Ter here has none of the sluggish appearance it does in Girona most of the year round.

🔥 Ripoll

The comfortable road descending from Camprodon to Ripoll (some 24 kilometres)

follows the timeless route taken by pilgrims and travellers from France. On the way, stop at the delightful village of **Sant Pau de Segúries** and at the **Monastery of Sant Joan de les Abadesses** (St. John of the Nuns). The fine light sculpture of the cloisters, betraying a French influence, contrasts with the massive effect of the interior. Note, too, the **Sant Misteri,** a remarkable sculptural group dating from 1250, full of life and movement.

The **Monestir de Santa Maria de Ripoll** (Monastery of St. Mary of Ripoll) is the Westminster Abbey of Catalonia, the key to the Romanesque Road, and the depository (with Montserrat) of the Catalan soul, its history and aspirations. Inside the church rest the bodies of Wifredo el Velloso (Wilfred the Hairy), Count of Barcelona and first ruler of an independent Catalonia; Berenguer III, who expanded the Catalan kingdom and built its navy; and Berenguer IV, the saint, who drove the Moors from their last toehold in his empire. Part of the church is being dug up to reveal even earlier foundations.

Begun in 879 on the orders of Wifredo el Velloso, the monastery, which served as a cementing factor for all Catalans, found itself in a strategic position on the cusp of Europe and Iberia and grew in importance as an exchange floor for ideas and learning between the two cultures. The decline of the Counts of Barcelona heralded its own decline for long centuries.

By 1835, the Monastery of Santa Maria had fallen into ruin. Only through the zeal and efforts of a certain Bishop Morgades, who took it in hand, was the building saved from complete devastation. Before the century's end, the weary prelate could contemplate the finished work and the monastery was reconsecrated.

Nothing at the monastery quite equals the magnificent 12th-century arched **doorway** leading into the church, described as "the Bible in stone" and "the triumphal Arch of Catholicism". More than 200 carved stone figures in seven horizontal bands tell the story of the Old and New Testaments. A superb example of genuine folk-art, it was carved to illustrate the Bible in an easily intelligible way to country people, many of them illiterate. To give the story immediacy and impact, each figure is carved wearing contemporary Catalan costume.

Another treasure here is Santa Maria's two-storeyed Romanesque **cloister,** built between the 12th and 14th centuries. The trapezoidal garden is surrounded by 252 columns (126 on each level), each with intricately carved capitals supporting 55 graceful arches.

Resplendent arched doorway graces Monastery of St. Mary of Ripoll.

The shafts of the older columns were fashioned from reddish jasper.

The **Església de Sant Pere** (St. Peter's Church) houses the Lambert-Mata Public Library and the Ripoll Archive

The change from warm, sea breezes to brisk, mountain air is felt at Camprodon, in its Pyrenean setting.

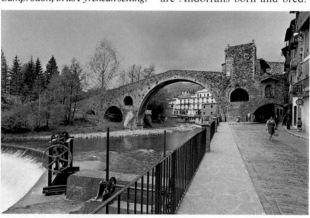

and Museum. The museum has an excellent collection of popular art, firearms, costumes, all sorts of household implements, rural worktools, ceramics and textiles, which provides a vivid general impression of Catalonian country life over the last centuries.

Andorra

Nobody can claim to have seen the world without a stop in Andorra, the Biggest Small Country in Europe (its own boast), a 187-square-mile political anachronism.

The principality huddles between mountain peaks in the Pyrenees, surrounded by Spain and France. Of a population of 26,000, a mere 8,000 are Andorrans born and bred.

The rest are immigrants attracted by the mountain air and… the income tax system. It's non-existent.

The shopping is a dream. After 700 years of fiercely defended independence, the country's spectacular scenery now takes second place; most of today's visitors are heading straight for the tax-free cameras, hi-fis and whisky in the bulging shops of Meritxell Street, in **Andorra La Vella,** the capital. Three million tourists pass through the town every year, mostly with bargains in mind.

In a nice compromise, official language of Andorra is Catalan. Spanish and French are almost universally understood, while English and German are most useful in the shops. French francs and Spanish pesetas are equally valid in Andorra. In practice, almost any foreign currency is recognized and accepted by the merchants. In smaller shops of Meritxell Street, bargaining is appropriate. Astute haggling should win a 10 per cent discount.

The country has no armed forces. It successfully escaped involvement in both World Wars and the Spanish Civil War. Though there is a 24-man police force, there's no jail. Crime is rare—unless you count a bit of smuggling as a mortal sin. The main job of the police force is slowing down the 10,000 duty-free Andorran cars zooming round the highways. Significantly, the state picks up a lot of revenue from traffic fines.

Since 1278, Andorra has been under the joint suzerainty of the Spanish bishop of nearby Urgel and the French Counts of Foix (now represented by the President of France). A feudal tithe still must be paid. In alternate years, the French President receives 900 francs, and the bishop collects 450 pesetas, six hams, 12 chickens and 24 cheeses.

Visit the Casa dels Valls (House of the Valleys), a 16th-century building in which the country's parliament and court are housed. The nation's archives rest in a chest secured with six locks, the keys to which are held in the six parishes.

In Andorra, there are more miles of trout streams than paved roads. Hunters enjoy nearly 80 square miles of game reserves, all alive with rabbit, hare, partridge and chamois. Some fine skiing is to be had at Grau Roig, Soldeu and Arinsal. There are curative springs in Les Escaldes.

And everywhere, peace and quiet.

Barcelona

The chances are your trip to Barcelona will only be a side trip or excursion from the Costa Brava.* Your time will then be limited and so the best idea is to make a tour of the compact old part of the town. If you can prolong your stay in the capital, there is no lack of other areas of interest: the modern city that grew up in the 19th and early 20th centuries, with long, straight and leafy avenues; the portside area, strong on atmosphere and local colour; Montjuïc, the mountain in southern Barcelona with everything from fairgrounds to museums, and reached by aerial cable-car.

Gothic Quarter

The nucleus of old Barcelona, the Barri Gòtic, is concentrated round the cathedral. Here are elements from just about every century since the Iberian tribesmen first settled on the site over 2,000 years ago.

On the spot where the cathedral stands today, the Romans dedicated a temple to Hercules (you will see three remaining columns in nearby Carrer del Paradis). Two early Christian basilicas stood on the same site before the construction of the present **Catedral de Santa Eulalia** between 1298 and 1454. Don't be taken in by the façade, however—it wasn't built until the end of the 19th century, when new work on the cathedral began, thanks to a subsidy from a rich industrialist. Some critics complain that he spoilt the pure Catalan Gothic effect. But don't worry about the critics. Come back, if you can, one night when the delicate spires are illuminated and light glows through the stained-glass windows from the inside. You can scarcely fail to be impressed.

The interior is laid out in classic Catalan Gothic form, with three aisles neatly engineered to produce an effect of grandeur and uplift. Impossibly slender columns soar upwards to support the nave; muted golden light filtering through 500-year-old stained-glass windows adds to the extraordinary effect of spaciousness—one of the most striking characteristics of Catalan Gothic architecture.

Below the altar, go down to the Crypt of St. Eulalia, the 13-

---

* Tourists settling in for over a day will find a complete guide to Barcelona in another book in this series, the Berlitz travel guide BARCELONA AND COSTA DORADA.

year-old martyr to whom this cathedral is dedicated. Explicit bas-relief carvings on the 14th-century alabaster sarcophagus supply vividly gruesome details of her torture and execution. Behind the altar, at the Chapel of the Holy Sacrament, have a look at the Christ of Lepanto. Juan de Austria carried this sacred image into the decisive sea battle of Lepanto (Spaniards and Venetians versus the Turks), and legend has it that the Christ image moved its body at precisely the right moment to escape a bullet.

At this point, a strange squawking will draw you out into the **cloister**—to be greeted by the sight of a pack of geese frolicking in a pool of water, surrounded by palm trees, green plants, a fountain and fine, pure Gothic architecture. Generations of their ancestors have also lived here.

Pride of the **Cathedral Museum,** with its religious paintings and sculpture from the 14th century onwards, is undoubtedly the *Piedad del Arcediano Desplá,* executed in 1490 by Bartolomé Bermejo on commission from an egocentric archdeacon, who is pictured kneeling in the foreground of this transcendental biblical scene.

A short walk down Carrer de la Tapineria—where cobblers made shoes called *tapín* —leads to Plaça de Berenguer el Gran. Behind the modern equestrian statue of Ramón Berenguer III (who ruled Catalonia from 1096 to 1131) stands a reconstructed Roman wall. You can follow the wall for a fair distance on either side of the Plaça de l'Ángel. Sections of this ancient fortification come to light in incongruous places: "Roman wall visible inside" boasts a notice outside one Gothic Quarter boutique.

In the nearby **Museu d'Història de la Ciutat** (Museum of City History), a converted 16th-century palace, there are paintings, tapestries, maps and documents of municipal import. But the real spectacle is below ground. Beneath this museum are the remains of a settlement the Romans called Julia Faventia Augusta Pia Barcino. You can follow the paths of that civilization around the foundations of the houses, a drainage system, roads, market-places. The well-lit, clearly documented archaeological zone now extends as far afield as the subsoil beneath the cathedral.

The museum windows face onto **Plaça del Rei** (King's

Square), where, in the Middle Ages, farmers sold their produce and locksmiths made bolts. In front, **Saló del Tinell** (Tinell Hall), where Columbus may have been welcomed by Ferdinand and Isabella on his return from America. The extraordinary span of the meeting hall's ceiling, without a column or support, represents a remarkable technical feat.

Beside the hall, the Archives of the Crown of Aragon house documents dating back to the 9th century and some very ancient books. The archives are off-limits to tourists—unless they can lay claim to being scholars.

Rooftops of Barcelona, old and new, viewed from Gaudí's Parc Güell.

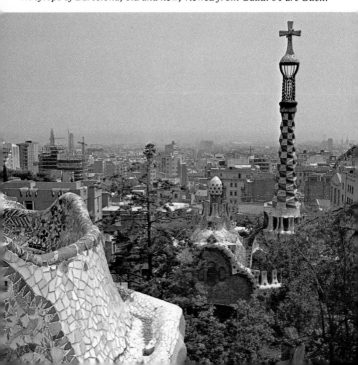

Two other absolutely major buildings of medieval civic architecture remain to be visited: the Generalitat (Provincial Council) and Casa de la Ciutat or Ajuntament (City Hall), facing one another on Plaça de Sant Jaume.

The **Generalitat,** seat of the Catalonia's autonomous government, is interesting not only for its stately architecture, but also for the striking details of its decoration (particularly sumptuous in the St. George's Room). You will never be allowed to forget St. George was the patron saint of Catalonia as well as of England, and the same figure is to be found all over the town. Upstairs, too, is a charming orange-tree courtyard.

The **Casa de la Ciutat** should be seen from Carrer de la Ciutat to appreciate the original 14th-century façade. The building still serves, from time to time, for ceremonial meetings and the impressive 14th-century Saló del Consell de Cent (Hall of the Council of One Hundred) does honour to any assembly.

La Rambla

La Rambla is a boulevard running east to west, a broad strip of throbbing life over a mile long bordered by two busy arteries. But La Rambla is more: it is an outdoor market, a caldron of gossip, a hotbed of café life, a thieves' den, a

The Sagrada Familia's spires symbolize Barcelona's architectural vitality.

lovers' rendezvous. Beneath the linking branches of La Rambla's plane trees, all the different elements of Barcelona fuse.

Every couple of cross-streets, the Rambla's character changes. So does its official name: Rambla dels Estudis, Rambla dels Caputxins, Rambla de Santa Mónica and the others—five in all—which explains why very often it's simply referred to as Les Rambles.

To walk down La Rambla's full extent from the Plaça de Catalunya to the Monument a Colom (Columbus Monument) is an experience, an entertainment and an education. You can buy a canary, a monkey, a mouse or a turtle; a carnation, an orchid, a potted plant or a bird-of-paradise flower, a packet of nuts or one cigarette from a news-stand. Here the bookstalls stock all the papers and magazines of Europe, gypsies insinuate hot watches, lottery sellers flutter tickets practically guaranteed to win you a million.

Visit the Frontón to see a game of *pelota* (called *jai-alai* in the Basque country). The ball flashes around the court at speeds of up to 125 miles per hour. The betting around you is even more frantic; split tennis balls stuffed with gaming slips whizz overhead. Or look at a peepshow—mostly of views of Barcelona.

Need a rest? Stop at one of the multitude of bars and cafés lining La Rambla while traffic streams by in a seemingly endless flow, barely noticed—except by the waiters, brandishing their trays aloft, who dodge to and fro to their sources of supply between serried ranks of cars.

Alternatively, leave bustling La Rambla, go through a small arcade and find yourself in the quiet, stately **Plaça Reial**, the city's finest square. Or simply hire a chair on the Rambla. People-watching is a cheap entertainment by any standards, and there's hours-worth to watch.

On the other side of La Rambla is the **Mercat de Sant Josep** (Market of St. Joseph, also known as Boqueria). Ease your way through the throngs of bustling housewives; your ears will ring with their strident shouts. Look at the eye-catching display of Mediterranean fish, fruit and vegetables. Mounds of pig trotters (pig's feet) share the space with piles of vegetables whose names are a treat in themselves—you may be at pains to find an English equivalent.

Just beside the market, the **Palau de la Virreina** is one of the most sumptuous buildings on the Rambla. It houses the city hall Department of Culture, as well as the Postal Museum and the Numismatic Cabinet, of great interest to specialists. Other floors of the palace are used for topical exhibitions.

One of the largest and most majestic opera auditoriums in the world, the **Gran Teatre del Liceu** hides behind a discreet façade further down La Rambla. And just off La Rambla, in Carrer Nou de la Rambla, stands **Palau Güell,** one of the grand houses built by Antoni Gaudí (1852–1926), an *art nouveau* architect born in the Catalonian market town of Reus.

South of Carrer Nou de la Rambla are the noisy streets of the infamous **Barri Chino** ("Chinatown"). Here, while prostitution was outlawed in Spain in 1956, the colourful denizens of Barri Chino's grubby bars have, one might gather, yet to be notified, and the area has a classic air of port-side low-life.

La Rambla, with its ebullience, colour and life, is the Barcelona that sticks in the mind long after the classic scenes have disappeared.

What to Do

Sports and Other Activities

Hot summers and mild winters make the Costa Brava a year-round sportsman's paradise. And with a coastline including long beaches, broad bays and scores of secluded coves, water sports are naturally the favourites. But there's plenty more to do. There are activities for everyone, ranging from the strenuous to the relaxed.

Sportsmen on the Costa Brava have one enemy: that friendly Mediterranean sun can be deceptive. If you aren't used to it, three or four hours of mid-afternoon heat can burn you a bright lobster-red. Sunburn is painful and a heavy dose can ruin a holiday, so do take the sun in easy stages—half an hour twice a day is plenty—until you have acquired some sort of tan. For the rest of the time, wear a T-shirt or something light to cover your shoulders and upper body. A hat is a good idea, too.

Here's a list of sports to choose from during a holiday on the Costa Brava:

Simple joys of sea, sun and sand are Costa Brava's priceless assets.

Boating

Most major beaches have some kind of water-craft for hire, and larger hotels fronting onto beaches may have sailing-boats available. Prices vary considerably from resort to resort.

Patines are two-seater craft propelled by a footdriven waterwheel. They are equipped with a rudder and are stable enough for a young child to be aboard in the company of an adult. Two adults and one child is the usual maximum load permitted. Beach concessionaires often don't watch weather conditions. Don't take a pedal boat out in a stiff seaward wind—you might end up in Italy!

Gondolas are flat-decked "banana-boat"-type canoes, which only provide seating for one, although two can have a lot of fun. Propulsion comes from a double-ended paddle. Gondolas tip easily, so are not suitable for younger children or non-swimmers.

Water-Skiing

Rising fuel costs mean that water-skiing is becoming an expensive way to whizz round the bay. All the more reason to double-check rival schools for length of runs, number of attempts allowed for "getting up" and discounts for multiple runs paid for in advance. Serious lessons are usually confined to the early morning, when the sea is calmest and most tourists are still in bed. For something less energetic, try powerboat parachuting. An on-shore wind, a dash of courage, and you'll be soaring heavenwards. You needn't even get your feet wet, and the view is superb.

Boardsailing

Boardsailing, also known as windsurfing—combining the speed of sailing with the thrill of tightrope walking—has come of age on the Costa Brava. Equipment and instructors are available in many resorts.

Snorkelling

An immensely popular sport in the clear waters of the Costa Brava. The rugged coastline conceals inaccessible coves except by scrambling down steep cliffs, or by boat. The basic law of snorkelling has it that the tougher the climb, the more secluded the spot, the bigger the fish—so with luck...

But there's lots of fun, too, snorkelling in quieter corners of resort beaches. In shallow water, try catching small octopus with your hands (leave them alone if you're out of your depth). You can eat them too: when you've brought one ashore, turn it inside out, pound it on a rock to soften it and dry it in the sun for 24 hours. Then slice it thinly, grill it over a charcoal fire and sprinkle it with lemon. Eat to the accompaniment of white wine.

lar—and cheapest—sport is obviously swimming. In peak season, major resort beaches are packed, but between towns you can find much less crowded strips. Catalonian beach facilities may not always be as good as in some other countries, though larger beaches have restaurants, showers and changing rooms. Beach-chairs can be hired for a daily fee.

Reasonably priced equipment is on sale in all resorts—from simple masks for children to sophisticated, high-powered spearguns for adults.

Swimming

With its long coastline, the Costa Brava's most popu-

The beach areas are usually not manned by life-guards (though some do have first-aid stations). So keep an even closer watch on children than you normally would, particularly on those rare beaches such as Platja de Pals, where there can be powerful waves. **75**

Fishing

Fishing from rocks along the coastline is popular, but results are better if you hire a boat and head for open water. Village fishermen who know local waters may be available for half-day or daily hire. You can negotiate most expeditions to include a stop at some isolated cove for a picnic lunch. The boat-owner, customarily, joins the picnic as the guest of his passengers. Cheap fishing tackle is available in most resorts.

There's abundant river fishing, also, in Girona Province. The rivers Ter and Onyar are well stocked with barbel, carp, tench and eel, while pike and carp are caught in Lake Banyoles. There's first-class trout fishing in government-controlled stretches along the River Segre. Licences are needed for river fishing. A special 15-day card for tourists (including trout licence) is available. Apply to ICONA (the government body concerned with wildlife preservation), including a passport-sized photograph and passport details:

Carrer Sabino de Arana, 22, Barcelona.

Golf

Girona Province offers golfers three courses:

Club de Golf de Pals, 18 holes, near Begur.

Club de Golf Costa Brava, 18 holes, at Santa Cristina d'Aro, near La Platja d'Aro.

Reial Club de Golf de la Cerdanya, 18 holes, 3 kilometres from Puigcerdà station

Lush golf green in Girona Province.

(in the north of the province, near the French frontier). The club has an office at: Rambla de Catalunya, 66, 3rd floor, Barcelona 7.

Horse Riding

Several ranches along the Costa Brava hire out horses. In addition, some resort travel agencies advertise riding excursions with transport to and from a ranch, a few hours of riding, and a country meal.

Hunting and Shooting

Very popular amongst Catalans who bag hare, rabbit, quail, duck and partridge. For details about hunting permits and laws concerning temporary import of firearms, check with local or foreign tourist offices, or write to ICONA (see p. 76).

Skiing

Three big ski resorts are located in the Pyrenees within 100 miles of the Costa Brava: La Molina, Masella and Nuria. La Molina lies 20 kilometres from Puigcerdá and only 15 kilometres from the French frontier. Snow fields cover nearly 20 square miles which include 17 marked runs. The outstanding Olympic run, suited to international competition, drops more than 2,700 feet over a distance of 8,100 feet. La Molina facilities include downhill and cross-country pistes, ski jumps, chair lifts, ski tows and over a dozen hotels. Best ski months are December to April. Full information from any tourist office or from the Direcció General de Turisme, which issues a detailed booklet on winter sports in Catalonia.

Tennis

Many hotels, apartments and villa-complexes have their own tennis courts, but due to a greater number of tennis players in summer, you may have to book a day ahead. Some hotels have professionals on staff who give lessons.

Pelota

A visit to Barcelona provides you with the chance to see this famed Basque ball-game (it's called *jai-alai* in the Basque country). Players sling the ball using wicker baskets at speeds up to 125 mph. At Principal Palacio, Plaça del Teatre, La Rambla, Barcelona. Games daily, usually starting at 5 p.m.

The Bullfight

If you've never seen a bull-fight, a Costa Brava holiday provides you with the chance. You may be repelled by the spectacle, you may swear never to return to it, or you may become a lifelong *aficionado*. Whatever your reaction, you'll have to admit that the *corrida,* Spain's national fiesta, is a unique, unforgettable experience.

The fight is divided into three *tercios* (thirds), each designed to tire the animal in preparation for its death. First, the bull charges into the ring and assistants play it with capes so that the matador can examine the way it moves, the direction in which it prefers to thrust with its horns. Then he takes over and tries the bull himself, using the big red and yellow cape. This is perhaps the most beautiful part of the fight; but every graceful pass is bringing the bull closer to the inevitable finale.

The second *tercio* is when the *picador,* the mounted spearman, uses his lance on the bull's huge shoulder muscles. This spearing has two purposes: it tires the bull and it forces him to drop his head into a position which will allow the matador to place his sword for the kill. The audience invariably boos the *picador,* not for any love of the bull, but because if the spear is used too much the bull will lose his strength and will to fight. After the *picador* comes the turn of the *banderilleros* who place darts in the bull's shoulder. Lodged correctly into his muscles, the darts counter any preference the animal may have for hooking with the left or right horn.

Finally comes the third *tercio* when the matador fights the bull with the small, dark-red *muleta.* Gradually he dominates the animal—even to the point where he can turn his back on it and walk casually away—and eventually comes the time known in English as "the moment of truth". With the bull theoretically completely under control, the matador sights along his sword and then lunges, leaning dangerously over the bull's horns to deliver the final thrust into a minute area between the shoulder blades.

Depending upon the quality and the bravery of the performance, the fight's *presidente* will indicate whether or not the matador is to be awarded an ear, two ears, or, after an exceptional performance, the tail of the animal he has killed. The crowd sometimes expresses its appreciation of the fight by waving handkerchiefs and tossing handbags, hats and wineskins *(botas)* into the ring.

The whole performance, consisting usually of six bulls killed by three matadors and their teams, lasts about two hours.

You may be sickened, fascinated or simply confused. A majority of foreigners are. But you will have witnessed a violent act which at times contains impressive beauty. With luck you'll begin to understand why in Spain this fantastic ballet of death is considered an art form.

On the Costa Brava, there is a choice of bullrings: at Lloret de Mar, Sant Feliu de Guíxols, Girona, Figueres, as well as two in Barcelona. The most outstanding performances are generally to be seen in Barcelona. Top matadors fight there in the summer.

Among several seating categories at the *corrida,* a good one is *sol y sombra,* which means you'll be in sun for part of the fight and shade for the rest. Seats are bare concrete, so it's a good idea to rent a cushion. Be on time, for in this domain, Spaniards are very punctual—rarely does a bullfight start late.

Tickets purchased in advance—those ordered through your hotel, for instance—cost 20 per cent more than the box-office price on the day of the fight. But the surcharge is worth the saving in queuing time, and tickets sold by street-hawkers are exorbitantly expensive.

Flamenco

Flamenco was born in Andalusia, in southern Spain, and that region remains the stronghold of the art. But in Barcelona and the bigger resort towns, you'll be able to visit a *tablao*—a floor show featuring guitar players, singers and dancers that at least gives something of the feel of flamenco—during your Costa Brava holiday. Flamenco is said to be Moorish in its origins, and certainly there's a resemblance to the wailing chants typical of Arab music.

There are two main groups of flamenco songs. One, bouncier and more cheerful, is the *cante chico* ("light song"). *Fandangos, sevillanas, bulerías, alegrías, malagueñas*—these are all part of the *cante chico*.

Cante chico themes are light, but they can also be touching.

The second group of songs is the *cante jondo* ("deep song"). Slow, piercing, nearly always brutally emotional, it deals with the intricacies and torments of love, death, the whole human predicament. It is the song of the great flamenco singers.

But you are highly unlikely to encounter any genuine *cante jondo*, although recordings abound; it's *cante chico* you'll hear at the *tablao flamenco*. These shows, which usually include a drink and a certain amount of audience participation, are staged in many tourist resorts.

The Sardana

The energetic yet graceful national dance of Catalonia, the *sardana*, with its haunting woodwind accompaniment, hypnotizes Catalans wherever they may be. The exact origins of this disciplined ring dance are unknown. But in the *Iliad*, Homer describes a Greek dance very like the *sardana*, and researchers suggest that Greeks may have introduced it to Catalonia when they were established in Empúries and elsewhere on the coast.

The modern *sardana* existed by the end of the 18th century, and in the 19th was revived after enthusiastic work by an Andalusian who lived in Figueres—José "Pep" Ventura. Amongst *aficionados* he's called Pep of the *tenora*, an allusion to a strident clarinet-like instrument played by the 11-man *cobla*, or band.

The deceptively simple-looking *sardana* is danced in normal everyday clothes, except on special occasions, and very often Catalans simply put their satchels, bags or briefcases in the centre of the circle. The dancers form a circle which grows as newcomers join it. If it proves unwieldy, they simply form another. If they run out of room, they make circles within circles. Each group has a leader who keeps meticulous time and signals changes. If he makes one error his ring loses its rhythm er; long-haired students join the same circle as middle-aged housewives. They may have little in common in everyday life, but the *sardana* reminds them that, whatever their social differences, they are Catalans. Even tourists can, technically, join in. In actual fact, prudence is advisable. There is a fairly strict rule that puts an end to most tourists' ambitions: no local would

and can't complete the final step in time with the band.

The wonder of the *sardana*, quickly noted by visitors, is the spirit it generates. The dance—performed in many resorts on weekend evenings—cuts all barriers. Doctors and farmers dance togeth-

Social barriers melt as Catalan national dance, sardana, *starts up.*

ever dare move into a circle that has a much higher standard of dancing than he is capable of, and the uninitiated visitor might thus find himself edged out. **81**

Shopping

Shopping Hours

Most Catalan shops are open from 9 a.m. to 2 p.m., and again from 4 to 8 p.m. Department stores open from 10 a.m. to 8 p.m. without a break for lunch, so for those not wishing or able to have a rest, it can be the least tiring moment to wander round these stores. In summer, shops in tourist resorts often stay open until 9.30 or 10 p.m. Bars and cafés are generally open without a break from 8 a.m. to midnight or later.

Best Buys

Perhaps the best buy in Spain today is footwear. Shoes and boots, both men's and women's, are of good quality leather. Though fashionable models are expensive, you can find bargains in everyday styles. (Shoes for children, though, can be more expensive than elsewhere.)

Items in leather and suede (sports jackets, full-length coats, handbags, etc.) remain among the best buys, but prices are rising.

Seasoned travellers know all about Spanish leather; but few realize that Spanish high fashion *(alta costura)* is slowly but surely edging in on the international market. Your resort boutique may not have much to offer in fashions, but in Barcelona, watch out for the big names.

While window-shopping on the Costa Brava, you may notice the high quality of children's clothing—and the unexpectedly high prices. If you want to dress your children like royalty, and can afford it, Spain is the place to buy.

Spirits and cigarettes are still a bargain by European and American standards. Top foreign-brand drinks, produced under licence in Spain, are sold for less than they cost at home; locally made cigarettes are also good value for money; a full range of imported Cuban cigars is available at prices considerably lower than in England, while quality Canary Island cigars are even cheaper.

Locally produced pottery and ceramics, colourful and decorative, or just utilitarian, make interesting gifts. Most resorts have at least one pottery shop, and some resorts are visited by salesmen leading donkeys laden with jugs and vases. Bargaining is acceptable with the latter.

Souvenirs

Thirty million tourists visit Spain annually (one to every Spaniard) and the souvenir industry strains to give them something new to buy. Most people, however, stick to the "traditional" Spanish souvenirs, such as bullfight posters (with or without your own name printed), bullfight swords, inlaid chess-sets, replicas of classic swords and pistols produced in Toledo, wrought-iron work or the typical Spanish *bota,* the soft leather wineskin.

More useful items, produced for local consumption as well as the tourist trade, are hand-made shawls, embroidered linen, lace-work, painted fans, hand-woven shopping baskets and many other items made of wickerwork and wood. Many of these objects are the work of craftsmen who, even in the face of Spain's recent dramatic entry into the 20th century, still pursue the age-old techniques of their fathers. (Industrialization only reached Spain with real force about 30 years ago.) But time's short...

Antiques

If you know what to look for, worthwhile antiques can be bought at bargain prices in Spain. You'll find antique shops in most larger resorts as well as in Girona, Barcelona and Besalú; but once an antique is inside a shop, the price goes skyhigh. Stroll through the streets by Bar-

Shopping anywhere in Spain is a happy venture for bargain-hunters. **83**

celona Cathedral and the triangle formed by Carrer de Portaferrissa, Carrer de Petritxol, Carrer del Pi. Search, too, at the weekly outdoor markets held in most villages and towns. Sometimes, gyp-

Fresh Mediterranean produce fills fruit-and-vegetable market stalls.

sies come in from the country with interesting, if battered, odds and ends for sale. You may find hand-carved wooden bowls, heavy iron keys, wrought-iron work, brightly painted tiles and, occasionally, tattered paintings and prints (which just might be worth something).

The flea market in Barcelona is at the Carrer del Dos de Maig, to the north of Plaça de les Glòries Catalanes (Monday, Wednesday, Friday and Saturday).

Where to Shop

Tourist centres may look like shopping paradises, but they rarely are. Some shops are excellent, but most tend to carry only lines with a proven turnover, so your choice is limited. And, in resort areas, prices are liable to be high.

So where should one shop? It's worthwhile keeping expensive purchases for a visit to Girona, Barcelona or larger inland towns. There you may get really excited by what you see, and you'll save 10, even 20 per cent, with a far wider choice. But, if you can't make it to one of the larger towns, don't worry; your resort, however small, will almost certainly be capable of supplying last-minute traditional buys or afterthoughts.

Although designed for tourists, the Poble Espanyol in Barcelona is a good place to pick up inventively designed objects, such as wickerwork baskets, carpets and bedspreads, as well as souvenirs.

Shopping Tips

Wherever you shop, try to compare prices of items in at least three stores before buying. Price control in Spain hasn't reached the sophisticated level of other countries. It's very much an open market, with few shops using the price-slashing ploy. And don't presume that because a shop is bigger its prices will be lower; one shop may blatantly overcharge, while the neighbouring store is perfectly honest.

Haggling is standard shopping practice at outdoor markets (though never at food stalls). Hard bargaining with gypsies is not only acceptable but essential to financial survival.

Tax Rebates for Visitors

The Spanish government levies a value-added tax (called ("IVA") on most items. Tourists from abroad will be refunded the IVA they pay on purchases over a stipulated amount. To obtain the rebate, you have to fill out a form, provided by the shop. The shop keeps one copy; the three others must be presented at the customs on departure, together with the goods. The rebate will then be forwarded by the shop to your home address.

To Market, To Market!

Market-day may be a world-wide custom; in the Mediterranean setting, however, it always has something quite special about it, and no less so in Catalonia. For the Catalans, market-day, whether it be the daily food mart or the weekly clothes and general market, is a time to buy and sell, a chance to gossip, an excuse to down a *copita* (glass) of sherry with friends.

Here's a list of market-days for main Costa Brava towns:

Monday: Blanes, Cadaqués, Torroella de Montgrí.

Tuesday: Lloret de Mar, Besalú, Caldes de Malavella, Castelló d'Empúries, Palamós.

Wednesday: Banyoles, Llançà.

Thursday: Tossa de Mar, Sant Feliu de Guíxols, L'Estartit, Figueres, Llagostera.

Friday: La Bisbal, El Port de la Selva.

Saturday: Girona.

Sunday: L'Escala, Palafrugell, Roses, Sant Feliu de Guíxols, Tordera (Barcelona Province).

Ferias and Festivals

Spain is the land of the *fiesta,* and the Costa Brava has its share of both religious and folk festivals. Information about exact dates and times of fiestas in your area can be requested at town halls or tourist offices. At tourist offices, ask for a copy of the "Spanish Tourist Calendar" booklet for Girona Province (to cover Spain, there are nine volumes), which lists all fiestas on the Costa Brava. Here are some outstanding annual events:

February

La Molina: Skiing championships.

March

In most larger towns: Holy Week observances. At its most spectacular in Girona, but more modest processions in other towns. Some villages present the Dance of Death when villagers dressed as skeletons dance to drum-beats. Other towns perform a Passion play, notably in Verges.

April

Figueres: Town fair, including an agricultural and industrial display, art exhibitions, bullfights and a flower battle.

May

Girona: Provincial flower show held in the beautiful cloisters of Sant Pere de Galligans Church, which houses the Archaeological Museum.

Ripoll: Town fair in honour of San Eudaldo. Dancing, cultural events and sports.

June

Palamós: Annual town fair, featuring folkloric and sports events.

Sant Pere Pescador: Events include water-skiing on the river and *sardana* dancing.

Tossa de Mar: Local fair featuring folkloric events.

July

Olot: An *aplec* (or reunion) of *sardana* dancers. Some 5,000 participants, including French Catalans, dance the *sardana* almost non-stop until well after midnight.

Calonge: Annual music festival.

L'Estartit, Palamós: Annual religious festivals, including a seaborne procession, fishing competitions, *sardana* dancing.

Lloret de Mar: The famous annual fair in honour of St. Christine (see p. 50). Fishing boats sail from Lloret to the beach beneath Santa Cristina Chapel. On the way, a wreath is thrown overboard in memory of those who have died at sea. The two-day festival includes folk dancing and has been declared of special interest to tourists.

Santa Cristina d'Aro, Blanes, Portbou, Sant Feliu de Guíxols, L'Estartit: Annual fairs including *sardana* dancing.

Cadaqués: Annual International Festival of Music and Painting.

Castell d'Aro: Annual Music Festival.

August

Pals: Festival of San Domingo, featuring *sardana* dancing.

El Port de la Selva: Local celebrations with *sardana* dancing and waterskiing contests.

La Platja d'Aro: Folkloric festival.

Sant Feliu de Guíxols: Major festival with folk dancing, sports and cultural events, bullfights, fireworks and prizes for the best sandcastles and sculptures made on the beach.

Torroella de Montgrí: Local festival with *sardana* dancing.

Llançà: Sardana and other folkloric dances as part of the local fair.

September

L'Escala: Local festivities, including the *sardana.*

Cadaqués: Local fair; *sardanas* and sports events.

Lloret de Mar: Local rural festival.

October

Sant Feliu de Guíxols: "Day of the Sea". Marine processions and *sardana* dancing.

Girona: Festival of San Narciso. Includes bullfights and horse shows.

November

Torroella de Montgrí: Festivities in honour of Santa Catalina. Includes *sardana* dancing.

Other Possibilities

Barbecues

Check at your hotel desk or at travel agencies to see if there's a barbecue *(barbacoa)* in your area—announcements of such events are usually posted on boards outside. For an all-in price, you can eat and drink as much as you like and, if you are still capable, dance. This is a good occasion for getting to know other like-minded visitors to the Costa Brava. Transport is provided.

Boat Trips

You can take boat trips from the beaches at most major Costa Brava resorts. Some last only an hour, others take you to a destination where you enjoy a picnic lunch before returning home. You'll be impressed by the dramatic sight of the Costa Brava coastline. The boats beach right on the sand, while swimmers clear the way.

Films

Most films are dubbed into Spanish. But in Girona and Barcelona some cinemas show films in original-language versions. Consult the entertainment sections of local newspapers for programmes.

Casino Gambling

After four decades of prohibition, casino gambling has been legalized in Spain. Casinos charge a small entrance fee and restrict admission to holders of an identity card or passport. Casinos on the coast include Casino de Lloret de Mar, Hotel Montecristo (Girona) and Castle of Peralada Casino.

Galleries and Museums

Several Costa Brava resorts have small museums which are mentioned in the WHERE TO GO section. Listed here are the more important museums or galleries in the province.

Figueres

Museu de l'Empordà (Empordà Museum) on the main square. Dedicated to the history and other aspects of the region. Well organized.

Teatre-Museu Dalí (Dalí Theatre-Museum). A museum as eccentric as its founder.

Empúries

Museu Arqueològic (Archaeological Museum). Large collection of Greek and Roman objects found on the site right beside the museum.

Girona

The **Museu Arqueològic Provincial** (Archaeological Museum) in Sant Pere de Galligans Church. Greek and Roman objects excavated at Empúries and some excellent paintings by artists such as Tintoretto and Murillo.

The **Museu de la Ciutat** (Museum of City History) in Carrer de la Força. Documents and objects relating to Girona's history.

Museu de la Catedral (Cathedral Museum) in the cathedral chapter-house. Among many interesting exhibits, two are outstanding: a 10th-century illuminated manuscript *(Book of the Apocalypse)* and a 12th-century tapestry.

Salvador Dali's museum in Figueres arouses many a heated debate.

Ripoll

Museu de Ripoll (Ripoll Museum) in Església de Sant Pere (St. Peter's Church). Remarkable collection of tools, clothing and household implements relating to country life. Also excellent collection of old handguns.

Wining and Dining

The Catalans appreciate hearty dishes based on honest ingredients fresh from the farm—and the sea. If you share this enthusiasm, some memorable treats are in store.

But to find native cooking, you'll have to escape from the tourist hotels, where the food tends towards a bland international compromise. Break the protective shield and sniff out the real places where the Catalans themselves are to be found.*

Since the Mediterranean is near at hand, the accent is on fish. Here are some traditional species you'll be offered—normally fried or simply grilled and served without a sauce. A tomato, onion and lettuce salad is usually offered as an optional side dish:

Lenguado—sole; *mero*—sea bass; *salmonetes*—Mediterranean red mullet; *calama-*

Dining under the ramparts of Tossa.

res—squid; *gambas*—prawns (shrimp); *langosta*—spiny lobster (seasonal and always expensive).

Two classic Spanish dishes, as popular in Catalonia as elsewhere, are *paella* and *gazpacho*.

Gazpacho is a tangy chilled soup made with tomatoes, green peppers, cucumbers, onions, croutons, oil, vinegar and spices. Many of the ingredients are served on the side and may be added to taste. It's been aptly described as "liquid salad" and makes an ideal first course to a fish dinner.

Paella, the best-known of all Spanish dishes, usually combines seafood and chicken, pork or rabbit, served on a base of saffron-coloured rice; peas, red peppers and anything else that takes the cook's fancy are also included. Normally served at lunchtime, the best *paellas* are always cooked to order, a process that takes at least half an hour.

But Catalonia has plenty of specialities of its own, e.g.:

A *zarzuela* is the Spanish version of an operetta, or mus-

ical comedy, and like a light-hearted musical, the dish of the same name offers a little of everything. It's a triumphant concoction of up to a dozen different kinds of seafood, including prawns, shrimp and clams, octopus, squid and various white fish, all topped by a brandy-and-wine sauce. It's mouth-watering, and filling.

Pollastre amb xamfaina: casseroled chicken served with an aubergine-and-tomato stew.

Butifarra: a rich, delicious pork sausage. It may come with chips and/or other vegetables, with eggs, or even an omelette, when it's called *tortilla ampurdanesa.*

Habas a la Catalana: broadbeans cooked with ham and *butifarra*. Sometimes only the broadbeans and ham are served, in which case the dish is eaten as an entrée.

The pastries of the Costa Brava will destroy your diet. Just look in a bakery window; you don't have to know the names of all the *tartas.* One is more delectable than the next, crowned with nuts, custard, dried fruits, meringue, chocolate or powdered sugar.

Crema catalana: a custard with a crisp, caramel-glaze topping.

---

* For more information on wining and dining in Spain, consult the Berlitz EUROPEAN MENU READER.

Restaurants

Spanish restaurants are officially graded by forks—one fork for the lowest grade, five forks for the top. But forks are awarded according to facilities available and the length of the menu, neither of which has anything to do with quality of the food. On the whole, three- and four-fork restaurants do serve good food, but two-fork establishments have a reputation amongst Spanish gourmets for giving excellent value.

Spanish restaurants often offer a *plato del día* (day's special or set menu). This is usually three courses with bread and wine at a stated price which depends on the restaurant's rating. Most set menu and *à la carte* prices include service, but in Spain a small tip is customary: 10 per cent is normally adequate. For more specific tipping recommendations, see p. 121 in the Blueprint section.

Most restaurants on the coast are open for lunch from 1–3 p.m. Dinner is normally served from 8 until 10 p.m. (or even later in larger towns).

A hint to keep costs down: order *vino de la casa* (house wine). You'll save half or two-thirds over the price of a bottled wine.

Beach Restaurants
(Merenderos)

Beach restaurants are scattered along the Costa Brava, and if you can't face returning to your hotel or are determined to spend the whole day at the beach, it's hard to beat them for convenience and atmosphere. Informality is the keyword; the waitress is as likely to be wearing a bikini as the customer. Menus are simple, but tasty and filling: *paella,* fish, omelette and the ubiquitous steak or chicken.

Bars and Cafés

These establishments are indispensable to the Spanish lifestyle. It has been suggested that if bars and cafés were suddenly to disappear, the Spanish economy would grind to a halt. It certainly does seem that more bright ideas are launched, more partnerships formed, more deals clinched in cafés than in offices.

Some cafés open at crack of dawn, catering to early-morning workers; most are open by 8.30 a.m. to serve breakfast. One of the pleasures of the Mediterranean is drinking an early-morning *café con leche* (white coffee) at an outdoor café while a town comes to life. The price of a coffee buys a seat at a table for as long as you care to stay.

Wines and spirits are served at all hours in Spanish bars and cafés. Bills include service, but small tips are customary. It's usually 10–15 per cent cheaper to take your coffee or aperitif standing at the bar.

The patrons at this typical open-air local café take their time as they catch up on the latest news.

Tapas

Tapas have been called Spain's greatest contribution to the world of food. A *tapa* is a bite-sized morsel: meat-balls, olives, fried fish, other sea-food, vegetable salad, mush-rooms grilled, then dipped in garlic sauce...a *tapa* can be almost anything.

The term derives from the old custom of giving a bite of food with a drink, the snack

Fishermen unload their day's haul, meaning fresh seafood at the table.

being served on a saucer (*tapa* means literally "lid") which covered the glass. Today, sadly, the custom of giving the *tapa* is all but dead, though the idea of selling it is stronger than ever. Some bars specialize in *tapas*, so instead of dining formally in a restaurant, you can fill up in a bar by eating your way down a long counter crammed with tastily prepared dishes. (Vocabulary: one helping is called a *porción;* a large serving is a *ración;* half as much, a *media-ración*.) But beware: you could end up spending more for a feast of *tapas* than for a conventional meal.

Wines and Spirits

The most famous of all Spanish wines is sherry, a wine fortified with brandy, which is matured and bottled in the Andalusian town of Jerez de la Frontera. There are five main types: *manzanilla*, very pale, light to the taste and dry; *fino*, also very pale but slightly heavier; *amontillado*, amber-coloured, medium-dry; *oloroso*, dark gold in colour and with a fuller body; *cream*, sweet, smooth and the most popular of all sherries.

Spanish table wines range from adequate to excellent. For cheaper wines, try those from Valdepeñas in central Spain. Many towns in Girona Province produce *vino corriente* (ordinary wine), as do some of the resort towns (Llançà's wines are highly considered). Perhaps the best of all

Gironese wines are those produced in the privately owned castle in Peralada; outstanding is *claustro,* a sparkling wine which experts claim is on a par with *gran codorníu* (produced in the Catalan town of Sant Sadurní d'Anoia). Other high-quality Spanish wines are the well-known reds from Rioja.

Spanish brandy can be a bit heavy and sweet, and takes some getting used to. However, there are infinite varieties and *aficionados* swear by it.

Spain is a bonanza for drinkers of all categories. Most brands of spirits are produced under licence in the country and remain inexpensive, despite recent price increases. Imported Scotch whisky is an outstanding exception. Locally produced whisky tends to leave connoisseurs unenthusiastic.

Sangría, the popular summer drink, is a mixture of red wine, lemonade, brandy and chopped fruit. Spaniards drink it in moderation as a refresher. Tourists who take it with their meals may find it too heavy and strong; ask to have it diluted with soda-water.

Breakfast

This comes last, because in Spain breakfast is such an insignificant meal, just an eye-opener to keep one alive until a huge and late lunch. A typical Costa Brava breakfast consists of a cup of coffee and past-

Outdoor cafés and restaurants are a focal point of Spain's social life.

ry. Breakfast coffee *(café con leche)* is half coffee, half hot milk. If it tastes too foreign to you, many bars and restaurants stock milder instant coffee as well. Also, in deference to foreign habits, *desayuno completo* is now available in most hotels and some cafés: orange juice, eggs, toast and coffee.

Returning to the subject of breakfast pastry, two types are worth a try. *Ensaimadas,* large fluffy sweet rolls dusted with sugar, are a breakfast idea from the Costa Brava's overseas cousins, the Balearic Islanders. If you can find them, don't miss trying *churros. Churros* are fritters, often made before your eyes by a contraption which shoots the batter into boiling oil. *Churros* served with a very thick, hot chocolate is also a very popular afternoon snack in Spain. Hot chocolate with cream is called *un suizo*—meaning, naturally, "a Swiss".

To Help You Order...

Could we have a table?	**¿Nos puede dar una mesa?**
Do you have a set menu?	**¿Tiene un menú del día?**
I'd like a/an/some...	**Quisiera...**

beer	**una cerveza**	milk	**leche**
bread	**pan**	mineral water	**agua mineral**
coffee	**un café**	napkin	**una servilleta**
condiments	**los condimentos**	potatoes	**patatas**
cutlery	**los cubiertos**	rice	**arroz**
dessert	**un postre**	salad	**una ensalada**
fish	**pescado**	sandwich	**un bocadillo**
fruit	**fruta**	soup	**una sopa**
glass	**un vaso**	sugar	**azúcar**
ice-cream	**un helado**	tea	**un té**
meat	**carne**	(iced) water	**agua (fresca)**
menu	**la carta**	wine	**vino**

...and Read the Menu

aceitunas	olives	guisantes	peas
ajo	garlic	helado	ice-cream
albaricoques	apricots	higos	figs
albóndigas	meatballs	huevos	eggs
almejas	baby clams	jamón	ham
anchoas	anchovies	judías	beans
anguila	eel	langosta	spiny lobster
arroz	rice	langostino	prawn
asado	roast	lenguado	sole
atún	tunny (tuna)	limón	lemon
bacalao	codfish	lomo	loin
besugo	sea bream	manzana	apple
bistec	beefsteak	mariscos	shellfish
boquerones	fresh anchovies	mejillones	mussels
caballa	mackerel	melocotón	peach
calamares	squid	merluza	hake
(a la romana)	(deep fried)	naranja	orange
callos	tripe	ostras	oysters
cangrejo	crab	pastel	cake
caracoles	snails	pescado	fish
cebollas	onions	pescadilla	whiting
cerdo	pork	pez espada	swordfish
champiñones	mushrooms	pimiento	green pepper
chorizo	a spicy pork sausage	piña	pineapple
		plátano	banana
chuleta	chops	pollo	chicken
cordero	lamb	postre	dessert
dorada	sea-bass	pulpitos	baby octopus
ensalada	salad	queso	cheese
entremeses	hors-d'oeuvre	salchichón	salami
estofado	stew	salmonete	red mullet
filete	fillet	salsa	sauce
flan	caramel mould	sandía	watermelon
frambuesas	raspberries	sopa	soup
fresas	strawberries	ternera	veal
frito	fried	tortilla	omelet
galletas	biscuits (cookies)	tostada	toast
		trucha	trout
gambas	shrimp	uvas	grapes
granadas	pomegranates	verduras	vegetables

BLUEPRINT for a Perfect Trip

How to Get There

If the choice of ways to go is bewildering, the complexity of fares and regulations can be downright stupefying. A reliable travel agent can suggest which plan is best for your timetable and budget.

BY AIR

Scheduled Flights

Barcelona airport is linked by regular flights from many European and certain overseas cities. Connecting service from cities throughout Europe and North Africa operates via Madrid's airport, which is the main point of entry to Spain for transatlantic and intercontinental travellers. The flight from London to Barcelona takes about 2 hours, from New York, approximately 8 hours.

Charter Flights and Package Tours

From the British Isles: Package tours (including flight, hotel and board) are the most popular ways of visiting the Costa Brava. Most travel agencies recommend cancellation insurance, a modestly priced safeguard; you lose no money if illness or accident force you to cancel your holiday.

From North America: Charter flights and package tours are available through airlines and travel agents. You'll also find package tours organized by private organizations, companies or church groups.

BY ROAD

The route from Paris is entirely toll motorway to Alicante.

By car ferry from the U.K. and Ireland: the principal routes link Dover and Folkestone with Calais, Boulogne, Dieppe and Dunkirk; also: Ramsgate with Dunkirk; Newhaven with Dieppe; Portsmouth with St. Malo, Cherbourg and Le Havre; Southampton with Le Havre and Cherbourg; Weymouth with Cherbourg; Plymouth with Roscoff; Rosslare, Ireland, with Le Havre and Cherbourg; Cork, Ireland, with Le Havre and Roscoff.

There are also long-distance ferry services between Plymouth and Santander in Northern Spain (a 24-hour trip). From Santander, follow the N 240 to Barcelona.

The hovercraft from Dover to Calais or Boulogne takes about 35 minutes and costs a little more than the ferry.

By bus: Express coach services operate between London and Barcelona as well as between other European cities and Barcelona, with frequent departures in summer. You can travel by coach as part of a package holiday from London.

BY RAIL

The *Barcelona-Talgo* links Paris with Barcelona in about 11½ hours. For most other connections you'll have to change trains at Portbou.

Once in Spain, the main railway service in the Costa Brava region starts at Portbou, near the frontier with France, and then heads southwards to Barcelona. Several motorcoach lines link the railway stations of Figueres, Flaçà, Girona, Caldes de Malavella with Blanes and other important towns and resorts on the Costa Brava.

Visitors from abroad can buy the *RENFE (Red Nacional de los Ferrocarriles Española,* the Spanish National Railways) *Tourist Card* for a reasonable price, valid for unlimited rail travel within the country for periods of 8, 15 or 22 days (1st and 2nd classes available).

The *Rail Europ S* (senior) card, obtainable before departure only, entitles senior citizens to purchase train tickets for European destinations at reduced prices.

Any family of at least 3 people can buy a *Rail-Europ F* (family) card: the holder pays full price, the rest of the family obtain a 50% reduction in Spain and 14 other European countries; the whole family is also entitled to a 30% reduction on Sealink and Hoverspeed Channel crossings.

Anyone under 26 years of age can purchase an *Inter-Rail* card which allows one month's unlimited 2nd-class travel.

People living outside Europe and North Africa can purchase a *Eurailpass* for unlimited rail travel in 16 European countries including Spain. This pass must be obtained before leaving home.

When to Go

From November through March—darkest winter in much of Europe—shirtsleeve sunshine is still to be found on the Costa Brava, with temperatures usually in the upper 50s (Fahrenheit) and seldom falling below the mid-40s.

Nevertheless, the normally balmy days may be interrupted by chill winds and that rare local phenomenon—rain.

From June to September, hot days with low humidity are only occasionally broken by cooler evenings. In March, April, May and October, temperatures are usually quite warm, and these are probably the best months for a Costa Brava visit, if you want to get away from the crowds.

		J	F	M	A	M	J	J	A	S	O	N	D
Air temperature (maximum)	F	55	57	63	66	73	79	86	84	79	70	63	55
	C	13	14	17	19	23	26	30	29	26	21	17	13
Air temperature (minimum)	F	36	37	41	46	52	59	63	63	59	52	43	37
	C	2	3	5	8	11	15	17	17	15	11	6	3
Sea temperature	F	55	55	55	57	61	68	72	73	72	68	61	57
	C	13	13	13	14	16	20	22	23	22	20	16	14
Hours of sunshine		147	164	184	205	245	255	302	262	206	178	159	137

All figures shown are approximate monthly averages.

Planning Your Budget

To give you an idea of what to expect, here's a list of average prices in Spanish pesetas. However, they must be regarded as *approximate*, as inflation creeps relentlessly up. Prices quoted may be subject to a VAT/sales tax (IVA).

Baby-sitters. 350–500 ptas. per hour.

Camping. *De luxe:* 450–550 ptas. per person per day, 2,000–3,000 ptas. for a tent or caravan (trailer). *3rd category:* 300–400 ptas. per person per day (reduction for children), 650–800 ptas. for a tent or caravan.

Car hire. *Seat Ibiza* 2,100 ptas. per day, 21 ptas. per km., 25,000 ptas. per week with unlimited mileage. *Ford Escort 1.1 L* 2,600 ptas. per day, 25 ptas. per km., 40,000 ptas. per week with unlimited mileage. *Ford Sierra 2.0* (automatic, air-conditioned) 4,700 ptas. per day, 47 ptas. per km., 54,000 ptas. per week. Add 12% VAT.

Cigarettes. Spanish brands 50–115 ptas. per packet of 20, imported brands 175 ptas. and up.

Entertainment. Cinema in Barcelona 450–500 ptas., in resorts 300–400 ptas. Theatre 700 ptas. and up. Flamenco nightclub 700 ptas. and up. Discotheque 900 ptas. and up. Museums 100–300 ptas. (many are free).

Hairdressers. *Man's* haircut 800–2,000 ptas. *Woman's* haircut, shampoo and set or blow-dry 2,000–4,000 ptas., permanent wave 3,000–4,000 ptas.

Hotels (double room with bath). ***** 10,000–18,000 ptas., **** 9,000–14,000 ptas., *** 6,000–8,000 ptas., ** 3,500–5,000 ptas., * 2,000–3,000 ptas.

Meals and drinks. Continental breakfast 250–400 ptas., *plato del día* from 550 ptas., lunch/dinner in good establishment 2,500 ptas. and up, beer 125–200 ptas., coffee 60–90 ptas., Spanish brandy 120 ptas. and up, soft drinks 110 ptas. and up.

Shopping bag. Loaf of bread 60 ptas., 250 grams of butter 325 ptas., dozen eggs 180 ptas., ½ kilo of steak 700 ptas., 250 grams of coffee 300 ptas., 1 litre of fruit juice 180 ptas., bottle of wine 250 ptas. and up.

Youth hostels. 650–900 ptas. per night.

An A–Z Summary of
Practical Information and Facts

A star (*) following an entry indicates that relevant prices are to be found on page 102.

Listed after some basic entries is the appropriate Spanish translation, usually in the singular, plus a number of phrases that should help you when seeking assistance.

AIRPORT *(aeropuerto).* The Costa Brava is served by Girona airport, 11 kilometres from the provincial capital of Girona. Taxis from the airport to Girona take about 20 minutes. From Girona there are bus services to all Costa Brava resorts. **A**

Travellers on scheduled international flights arrive at Barcelona airport, well supplied with porters, currency-exchange offices, a tourist information office and car-hire firms. Trains link the airport with central Barcelona.

Porter!	**¡Mozo!**
Where's the bus for …?	**¿De dónde sale el autobús para …?**

CAMPING*. Catalonia and the Costa Brava are extremely popular with campers, and there are some 300 official sites in Catalonia, dotted up and down the length of the coast and inland. They are all listed in the brochure *Catalunya Campings,* available from the Federació Catalana det Campings: **C**

Via Laietana, 59, Barcelona; tel. 317 4416

Camping grounds are divided into four categories (luxury, 1st, 2nd and 3rd class), and rates and facilities vary accordingly. All sites, however, have electricity, drinking water, toilets and showers, and are under surveillance night and day.

For a complete list of campsites throughout the whole of Spain, consult any Spanish National Tourist Office (see TOURIST INFORMATION OFFICES).

May we camp here?	**¿Podemos acampar aquí?**
We have a tent/caravan (trailer).	**Tenemos una tienda de camping/ una caravana.**

What's the charge …?	¿Cuál es el precio …?
per day	**por día**
per person/child	**por persona/niño**
for a car/tent/caravan	**por coche/tienda/caravana**

CAR HIRE* *(coches de alquiler)*. See also DRIVING. There are car hire firms in tourist resorts and main towns. You'll find many types of cars for hire, but the most common is the Seat. Ask for any available seasonal deals.

Unless payment is made with a major credit card, a deposit, as well as advance payment of the estimated rental charge, is generally required. A small tax is added to the total bill. Third-party insurance is automatically included.

Normally you must be over 21 and hold an international driving licence. In practice, British, American and European licences are accepted in almost all situations.

I'd like to rent a car tomorrow.	**Quisiera alquilar un coche para mañana.**
for one day/a week	**por un día/una semana**
Please include full insurance coverage.	**Haga el favor de incluir el seguro a todo riesgo.**

CIGARETTES, CIGARS, TOBACCO *(cigarrillos, puros, tabaco)*. Spanish cigarettes can be made of strong, black tobacco *(negro)* or light tobacco *(rubio)*.

Ducados are popular for filtered black tobacco; *Fortuna, Nobel* (filter) and *Bisonte* (non-filter) are similar to foreign light brands. Nearly all popular foreign makes are available at twice to three times the price of the domestic product.

Locally made cigars are passable and cheap; among the better cigars, those from the Canary islands are excellent. Cuban cigars are available nearly everywhere. Most visitors to Spain consider local pipe tobacco a little rough.

A packet of cigarettes/ A box of matches.	**Un paquete de cigarrillos/ Una caja de cerillas.**
filter-tipped	**con filtro**
without filter	**sin filtro**
light tobacco	**tabaco rubio**
dark tobacco	**tabaco negro**

CLOTHING. From June to September the days are always hot, but evenings sometimes turn cool, so take a jacket or cardigan. During the rest of the year evenings are often chilly, and an unseasonably cold wind, the *tramontana*, can upset the benign climate, particularly in the northern part of the Costa Brava.

The days are long gone when Spanish authorities banned bikinis and made men wear bathing-suit tops. Spanish girls are as much at home in bikinis on the beach now as the foreigners. Topless bathing, too, is quite common on some stretches of beach. In spite of the up-heaval in Spain since General Franco's death, and the general realign-ment of attitudes, fundamental codes of behaviour change slowly, and discretion should be used as to when and where topless bathing is practised.

Sober clothing—no shorts or miniskirts—should, of course, be worn when visiting churches.

Will I need a jacket and tie?	**¿Necesito chaqueta y corbata?**
Is it all right if I wear this?	**¿Voy bien así?**

COMMUNICATION

Post offices are for mail and telegrams; usually you can't make tele-phone calls from them.

Hours vary slightly from town to town, but routine postal business is generally transacted: from 9 a.m. to 1 or 1.30 p.m. and 4 to 6 or 7 p.m., Monday to Saturday except for Saturday afternoons.

Postage stamps *(sello)* are also on sale at tobacconists' *(tabacos* or *estanco)* and often at hotel desks.

Mailboxes are yellow.

Poste restante (general delivery): If you don't know in advance where you'll be staying, you can have your mail addressed to *Lista de correos* (poste restante or general delivery) in the nearest town:

> Mr. John Smith
> Lista de correos
> Palamós
> Spain

Take your passport to the post office as identification.

Telegrams: Usual hours for telegrams: 8 a.m.–midnight. The main telegraph office in Girona:

C Avinguda Ramón Folch; tel.: 20 18 40 and 20 22 96 is open 24 hours a day.

Your hotel receptionist will also handle telegrams for you.

Night letters or night-rate telegrams *(telegrama de noche)* are delivered the following morning and cost much less than straight-rate messages.

Telephone. You can make local and international calls from public telephone booths in the street, from most hotels (often with heavy surcharges) and from some post offices. Area codes for different countries are given in the telephone directory. You'll need a supply of small change. For international direct dialling, pick up the receiver, wait for the dial tone, then dial 07, wait for a second sound and dial the country code (U.K. 44, Canada/U.S.A. 1), city code and subscriber's number.

To reverse the charges, ask for *cobro revertido.* For a personal (person-to-person) call, specify *persona a persona.*

Where is the (nearest) post office?	**¿Dónde está la oficina de correos más cercána?**
Have you received any mail for …?	**¿Ha recibido correo para …?**
A stamp for this letter/ postcard, please.	**Por favor, un sello para esta carta/tarjeta.**
express (general delivery)	**urgente**
airmail	**vía aérea**
registered	**certificado**
I want to send a telegram to …	**Quisiera mandar un telegrama a …**
Can you get me this number in …?	**¿Puede comunicarme con este número en …?**

COMPLAINTS. Tourism is Spain's leading industry and the government takes complaints from tourists very seriously.

Hotels, campsites and restaurants: The great majority of disputes are attributable to misunderstandings and linguistic difficulties, and should not be exaggerated. As your host wants to keep both his reputation and his licence, you'll usually find him amenable to reason. In the event of a really serious and intractable problem, you may demand an official complaint form *(Hoja Oficial de Reclamación/Full Oficial de*

Reclamació), which all hotels, campsites and restaurants are required by law to have available. The original of this triplicate document should be sent to the regional office of the Ministry of tourism; one copy stays with the establishment against which the complaint is registered, while the final copy remains in your hands as a record. Merely asking for a complaint form is usually enough of a threat to resolve most matters.

In the rare event of major obstruction, when it is not possible to call in the police, write directly to the Secretaría de Estado de Turismo:

Duque de Medinaceli, 2, Madrid

Bad merchandise and car repairs: New legislation has been introduced that greatly strengthens the consumer's hand. Public information offices are being set up, controls carried out, and fallacious information made punishable by law. For a tourist's needs, however, the tourist office, or in really serious cases, the police would normally be able to handle or, at least, to advise where to go.

CONSULATES *(consulado).* Most western European countries have consular offices in Barcelona. If you have trouble with the authorities or the police, consult your consulate for advice.

Canada: Via Augusta, 125, Barcelona; tel.: 301 55 85.

Great Britain*: Avinguda Diagonal, 477, Edificio Torre de Barcelona, 13th floor, Barcelona; tel.: 322 21 51.

Eire: Gran Via Carles III, 94 Barcelona; tel.: 330 96 52.

U.S.A.: Via Laietana, 33, Barcelona; tel.: 319 95 50.

South Africa: Gran Via de les Corts Catalanes, 634, Barcelona; tel.: 318 92 52.

Where's the ... consulate?	**¿Dónde está el consulado**
British/American	**británico/americano?**
Canadian/Irish	**canadiense/irlandés?**
South African	**sudafricano?**
It's very urgent.	**Es muy urgente.**

---

* Also for citizens of Commonwealth countries.

CONVERTER CHARTS. For fluid and distance measures, see page 110. Spain uses the metric system.

C **Temperature**

°C

°F

Length

cm

inches

meters

ft./yd.

Weight

grams

ounces

COURTESIES. See also MEETING PEOPLE. Politeness and simple courtesies still matter in Spain. A handshake on greeting and leaving is normal. In Catalonia, you should preferably begin the conversation, whether with a friend, shop girl, taxi-driver, policeman or telephone operator with a *bon dia* (good morning) or *bona tarda* (good afternoon). Always say *adéu* (goodbye or, oddly enough, hi/hallo, said at any time of the day) or, at night, *bona nit* when leaving. *Si us plau* (please) should begin all requests.

CRIME and THEFT. Spain's crime rate has caught up with the rest of the world. Thefts and break-ins are now common occurences. Hang on to purses and wallets, especially in busy places—the bullfight, open-air markets, fiestas. Don't take valuables to the beach. Lock cars and never leave cases, cameras, etc., on view. In Barcelona, tourists are a target for bag snatchers and the like—especially along the Ramblas and in the notorious Barri Chino. So be on your guard. If you suffer a theft or break-in, report it to the Guardia Civil. In Barcelona, go to your consulate where you will fill in a form that you then present at the police station *(comisaría)*.

I want to report a theft.	**Quiero denunciar un robo.**
My ticket/wallet (purse)/ passport has been stolen.	**Me han robado mi billete/cartera (monedero)/pasaporte.**

DRIVING IN SPAIN. To take your car into Spain, you should have: **D**

- an International Driving Permit (not obligatory for citizens of most Western European countries—ask your automobile association—but recommended in case of difficulties with the police as it carries a text in Spanish) or a legalized and certified translation of your driving licence
- car registration papers
- Green Card (an extension to your regular insurance policy, making it valid for foreign countries)

Also recommended: With your certificate of insurance, you should carry a bail bond. If you injure somebody in an accident in Spain, you can be imprisoned while the accident is under investigation. This bond will bail you out. Apply to your automobile association or insurance company.

A nationality sticker must be prominently displayed on the back of your car. Seat belts are compulsory. Not using them outside towns makes you liable to a stiff fine. A red reflecting warning triangle is compulsory when driving on a motorway (expressway). Motorcycle riders and their passengers must wear crash helmets.

Driving conditions: Drive on the right. Overtake (pass) on the left. Yield right-of-way to all traffic coming from the right. Spanish drivers tend to use their horn during daytime or lights at night when passing other vehicles.

Main roads are adequate to very good and improving all the time. Secondary roads can be bumpy. The main danger of driving in Spain comes from impatience, especially on busy roads.

Spanish truck and lorry drivers will often wave you on (by hand signal or by flashing their right directional signal) if it's clear ahead.

Note that on motorways in Catalonia the word for exit is *sortida,* while in the rest of Spain it is *salida.*

Parking and driving in Barcelona, like most major cities unless you really know your way about, are not much fun. Streams of heavy traffic roar down long, straight avenues, carrying all before them (including you, probably). And beware of horrendous traffic jams on Sunday evenings as the crowds return from the beach.

Speed limits: 120 k.p.h. (75 m.p.h.) on motorways, 100 k.p.h. (62 m.p.h.) or 90 k.p.h. (56 m.p.h.) on other roads, 60 k.p.h. in towns and built-up areas. Cars towing caravans (trailers) are restricted to 80 k.p.h. (50 m.p.h.) on the open road.

D **Parking:** Many towns charge a token fee for parking during working hours; the cities more. The attendants are often disabled, and it's usual to round off the price of the ticket upwards.

It is forbidden to park the car facing oncoming traffic.

Traffic police: Spanish roads are probably the best patrolled in all Europe. The men who do the patrolling are the motorcycle police of the Traffic Civil Guard *(Guardia Civil de Tráfico)*. They always ride in pairs and are always armed. They are extremely courteous at helping you find your way, are efficient with minor mechanical problems and go out of their way to help you if you have a breakdown. They are also tough on lawbreakers.

The most frequent offences include: speeding, travelling too close to the car in front, overtaking (passing) without flashing your direction indicator lights, travelling at night with a burnt-out light (Spanish law requires you to carry a complete set of spare bulbs at all times), failing to come to a complete halt at a STOP sign. Fines are payable on the spot.

Fuel and oil: Service stations, once sparsely dotted around the countryside, are now plentiful, particularly in tourist areas, but it's a good idea to keep an eye on the gauge in deserted areas.

All fuel is sold through the government monopoly, *Campsa,* and is available in super (97 octane), normal (92 octane), leadfree (still rare; 95 octane) and diesel. It's customary to give a coin or two as a tip.

Fluid measures

Distance

Breakdowns: Spanish garages are as efficient as any, but in tourist areas major repairs may take several days because of the heavy workload. Spare parts are readily available for all major makes of cars.

Road signs: Most road signs are the standard pictographs used throughout Europe. However, you may encounter these written signs:

¡Alto!	Stop!
Aparcamiento	Parking
Autopista (de peaje/peatge)	(Toll) motorway (expressway)
Ceda el paso	Give way (Yield)
Cruce peligroso	Dangerous crossroads
Cuidado	Caution
Despacio	Slow
Desviación	Diversion (Detour)
Peligro	Danger
Prohibido adelantar	No overtaking (passing)
Prohibido aparcar	No parking
Puesto de socorro	First-aid post

(International) Driving Licence	**carné de conducir (internacional)**
Car registration papers	**permiso de circulación**
Green Card	**carta verde**
Are we on the right road for...?	**¿Es ésta la carretera hacia...?**
Full tank, please.	**Llene el depósito, por favor.**
normal	**normal**
super	**super**
leadfree	**sin plomo**
Check the oil/tires/battery.	**Por favor, controle el aceite/ los neumáticos/la batería.**
I've had a breakdown.	**Mi coche se ha estropeado.**
There's been an accident.	**Ha habido un accidente.**

DRUGS. Until the 1980s, Spain had one of the strictest drug laws in Europe. Then possession of small quantities for personal use was legalized. Now the pendulum has swung back in the other direction: possession and sale of drugs is once again a criminal offence in Spain.

ELECTRIC CURRENT *(corriente eléctrica)*. Today 220-volt A.C. is becoming standard, but older installations of 125 volts can still be found. Check before plugging in. If the voltage is 125, American appliances (e.g. razors) built for 60 cycles will run on 50-cycle European current, but more slowly.

What's the voltage—125 or 220?	**¿Cuál es el voltaje—ciento veinticinco (125) o doscientos veinte (220)?**
an adaptor/a battery	**un adaptador/una pila**

E **EMERGENCIES.** Being thoroughly familiar with local conditions, your hotel receptionist or a taxi driver can be of great help. Depending on the nature of the emergency, refer to the separate entries in this section such as CONSULATES, MEDICAL CARE, POLICE, etc.

Though we hope you'll never need them, here are a few key words you might like to learn in advance:

Careful	**Cuidado**	Police	**Policía**
Fire	**Fuego**	Stop	**Deténgase**
Help	**Socorro**	Stop thief	**Al ladrón**

ENTRY and CUSTOMS FORMALITIES *(aduana).* Most visitors need only a valid passport to visit Spain, and even this requirement is waived for the British, who may enter on the simplified Visitor's Passport. Though residents of Europe and North America aren't subject to any health requirements, visitors from further afield should check with a travel agent before departure in case inoculation certificates are called for.

The following chart shows customs allowances for certain items of personal use.

Into:	Cigarettes		Cigars		Tobacco	Spirits	Wine
Spain 1)	300	or	75	or	350 g.	1.5 l. and 5 l.	
2)	200	or	50	or	250 g.	1 l. or 2 l.	
Australia	200	or 250 g. or			250 g.	1 l. or 1 l.	
Canada	200	and	50	and	900 g.	1.1 l. or 1.1 l.	
Eire	200	or	50	or	250 g.	1 l. and 2 l.	
N.Zealand	200	or	50	or	250 g.	1.1 l. and 4.5 l.	
S.Africa	400	and	50	and	250 g.	1 l. and 2 l.	
U.K.	200	or	50	or	250 g.	1 l. and 2 l.	
U.S.A.	200	and	100	and	3)	1 l. or 1 l.	

1) Visitors arriving from EEC countries
2) Visitors arriving from other countries.
3) A reasonable quantity.

Currency restrictions. Tourists may bring an unlimited amount of
112 Spanish or foreign currency into the country. Departing, though, you

must declare any amount beyond the equivalent of 500,000 pesetas. Thus if you plan to carry large sums in and out again it's wise to declare your currency on arrival as well as on departure.

I've nothing to declare.	**No tengo nada que declarar.**
It's for my personal use.	**Es para mi uso personal.**

FIRE *(incendio)*. Forest fires are a real menace during the scorching summers in Catalonia, so be very careful where you throw your cigarette butts. If you are camping, make sure your fire is extinguished before you move.

GUIDES and INTERPRETERS. Local tourist offices, hotels and travel agencies can put you in touch with qualified guides and interpreters if you want a personally directed tour or help in business negotiations.

We'd like an English-speaking guide.	**Queremos un guía que hable inglés.**
I need an English interpreter.	**Necesito un intérprete de inglés.**

HAIRDRESSERS* *(peluquería)*/**BARBERS** *(barbería)*. Most large hotels have their own salons and the standard is generally very good. Prices are far lower in neighbourhood salons in the towns than in the resorts and chic hotels. For tipping suggestions, see TIPPING.

The following vocabulary will help:

I'd like a shampoo and set.	**Quiero lavado y marcado.**
I want a ...	**Quiero ...**
haircut	**un corte de pelo**
razor cut	**un corte a navaja**
blow-dry (brushing)	**un modelado**
permanent wave	**una permanente**
colour rinse/hair-dye	**un reflejo/un tinte**
manicure	**una manicura**
Don't cut it too short.	**No me lo corte mucho.**
A little more off (here).	**Un poco más (aquí).**

H **HITCH-HIKING** *(auto-stop)*. In Spain, hitch-hiking is permitted everywhere. If you sleep out in the open, don't stay too close to camping and caravan (trailer) sites. Police passing the campsite may awaken you to check your identity.

Can you give me/us a lift to ...?	**¿Puede llevarme/llevarnos a ...?**

HOTELS and ACCOMMODATION*. Spanish hotel prices are no longer government-controlled. Accommodation ranges from simple rooms in a *pensión* (boarding house) to the luxurious surroundings of a five-star hotel. Before the guest takes the room, he fills out a form indicating the hotel category, room number, price and signs it. Breakfast is normally included in the room rate.

When you check into your hotel you might have to leave your passport at the desk. Don't worry, you'll get it back in the morning.

Other forms of accommodation:

Hotel-Residencia and **Hostal:** Modest hotels, often family concerns, also graded by stars (one to three).

Pensión: Boarding houses, graded one to three, with few amenities.

Fonda: Village inns, clean and unpretentious.

Parador: Of special interest to motorists, since usually located outside towns, often in very old or historic buildings. State-run.

Albergue: Wayside inns; stay limited to two nights. Also state-run.

Refugio: Mountain hunting lodges.

Albergue de Juventud: In the Costa Brava area there is one in Arenys de Mar and another in Barcelona. A youth-hostel membership card is required.

Residencia: When referred to as *hostal-residencia* or *hotel-residencia*, this term indicates a hotel without a restaurant.

I'd like a single/double room.	**Quisiera una habitación individual/doble.**
with a bath/shower	**con baño/ducha**
with a balcony/view	**con balcón/vista**
What's the rate per night?	**¿Cuál es el precio por noche?**

HOURS. To accommodate the midday pause, most shops and offices open from 9 a.m. to 2 p.m. and then from 4 p.m. to 8 p.m. or later. Restaurants start serving lunch about 1 p.m. and dinner between 8 and 10 p.m.

LANGUAGE. The official language of Spain, Castilian, is understood everywhere on the Costa Brava. However, a related Romance language, Catalan, is the native language of the people of Catalonia. Since the death of General Franco, there has been an immense increase in the use of Catalan, and many Catalans express themselves more freely—and more willingly—in Catalan than in Spanish. On a brief visit to the Costa Brava, your elementary Spanish will suffice, even if a few words of Catalan will always be appreciated.

For geographical reasons, the French language is widely understood and admired in Catalonia. In tourist areas, English and German are spoken as well. See also MAPS AND STREET NAMES.

	Catalan	Castilian
Good morning	*Bon dia*	*Buenos días*
Good afternoon/evening	*Bona tarda*	*Buenas tardes*
Good night	*Bona nit*	*Buenas noches*
Please	*Si us plau*	*Por favor*
Thank you	*Gràcies*	*Gracias*
You're welcome	*De res*	*De nada*
Good-bye	*Adéu*	*Adiós*

The Berlitz phrase book, SPANISH FOR TRAVELLERS, covers most situations you are likely to encounter in your travels in Spain. The Berlitz-Spanish-English/English-Spanish pocket dictionary contains some 12,500 concepts, plus a menu-reader supplement.

Do you speak English?	**¿Habla usted inglés?**
I don't speak Spanish.	**No hablo español.**

LAUNDRY and DRY-CLEANING. Most hotels will handle laundry and dry-cleaning, but they'll usually charge more than a laundry *(lavandería)* or a dry-cleaners *(tintorería)*.

I want these clothes cleaned/washed.	**Quiero que limpien/laven esta ropa.**
When will it be ready?	**¿Cuándo estará lista?**
I must have this for tomorrow morning.	**La necesito para mañana por la mañana.**

L LOST PROPERTY. The first thing to do when you discover you've lost something is obviously to retrace your steps. If nothing comes to light, report the loss to the Municipal Police or the Guardia Civil.

I've lost my wallet/handbag/ passport.

He perdido mi cartera/bolso/ pasaporte.

M MAPS and STREET NAMES. See also LANGUAGE. Since General Franco died, Spain has been undergoing a formidable upheaval in many domains. One manifestation is in the names of streets, many of which are being re-baptised, causing a tourist considerable confusion. We have tried to give the "new" names wherever possible, but if you can't find a certain street you're looking for, don't fret too long—far better ask.

Place and street names in Catalonia are mostly met with today in their Catalan versions: former Rosas is now seen as Roses, Ampurias as Empúries, etc.

A tip to help recognize the Catalan street signs:

Castilian	English	Catalan
Avenida	Avenue	*Avinguda*
Calle	Street	*Carrer*
Callejón	Alley/Lane	*Carreró*
Camino	Way/Road	*Camí*
Iglesia	Church	*Església*
Palacio	Palace	*Palau*
Pasaje	Passageway	*Passatge*
Paseo	Boulevard	*Passeig*
Plaza	Square	*Plaça*

The maps in this guide were prepared by Falk-Verlag, which also publish a detailed map of Barcelona.

I'd like a street plan of ...

Quisiera un plano de la ciudad de ...

a road map of this region

un mapa de carreteras de esta comarca

MEDICAL CARE. By far the best solution, to be completely at ease, is to take out a special health insurance policy to cover the risk of illness and accident while on holiday. Your travel agent can also fix you up with Spanish tourist insurance (ASTES), but it is a slow-moving process. ASTES covers doctor's fees and clinical care.

Health care in the resort areas and in the major cities is good. Most of the major resort towns have private clinics; the cities and rural areas are served by municipal or provincial hospitals.

For minor ailments, visit the local first-aid post *(casa de socorro)*. Away from your hotel, don't hesitate to ask the police or a tourist information office for help. At your hotel, ask the staff to help you.

Farmacias (chemists' shops, drugstores) are usually open during normal shopping hours. After hours, at least one per town remains open all night, called *farmacia de guardia,* and its location is posted in the window of all other *farmacias.*

Where's the nearest (all-night) pharmacy?	**¿Dónde está la farmacia (de guardia) más cercana?**
I need a doctor/dentist.	**Necesito un médico/dentista.**
I've a pain here.	**Me duele aquí.**
sunburn	**quemadura de sol**
sunstroke	**una isolación**
a fever	**fiebre**
an upset stomach	**molestias de estómago**
insect bite	**una picadura de insecto**

MEETING PEOPLE. The Spanish, as a whole, are one the world's most open and hospitable peoples, easy to talk to and approach, generous to a fault.

You might on occasions find the noise-level of a conversation somewhat deafening. What you perhaps take for a quarrel is more often than not simply news and gossip being transmitted... passionately.

The Spanish have their own pace. Not only is it bad manners to try to rush them, but unproductive as well.

MONEY MATTERS

Currency: The monetary unit of Spain is the *peseta* (abbreviated *pta.*).
Coins: 1, 5, 10, 25, 50, 100, 200 pesetas.
Banknotes: 200, 500, 1,000, 2,000, 5,000, 10,000 pesetas.

A 5-peseta coin is traditionally called a *duro,* so if someone should quote a price as 10 duros, he means 50 pesetas. For currency restrictions, see ENTRY AND CUSTOMS FORMALITIES.

M **Banks** are open from 9 a.m. to 2 p.m. Monday to Friday (Saturday 9 a.m. to 1 p.m.).

All banks are closed on Sundays and holidays—and watch out for those obscure holidays which occur so frequently in Spain!

Outside normal banking hours, many travel agencies, major hotels and other businesses displaying a *cambio* sign will change foreign currency into pesetas. The exchange rate is less favourable than in the banks. Banks and exchange offices pay slightly more for traveller's cheques than for cash. Always take your passport with you for identification when you go to exchange money.

Credit cards: All the internationally recognized cards are accepted by hotels, restaurants and businesses in Spain.

Eurocheques: You'll have no problem settling bills or paying for purchases with Eurocheques.

Traveller's cheques: In tourist areas, shops and all banks, hotels and travel agencies accept them, though you are likely to get a better rate of exchange at a national or regional bank. Remember always to take your passport along if you expect to cash a traveller's cheque.

Paying cash: Although many shops and bars will accept payment in sterling or dollars, you're best off paying in pesetas. Shops will give you less than the bank rate for foreign currency.

Prices: The cost of living remains somewhat lower than in most other European countries and North America.

Some prices are listed on page 102 to give you an idea of what things cost.

Where's the nearest bank/ currency exchange office?	**¿Dónde está el banco/la oficina de cambio más cercana?**
I want to change some pounds/ dollars.	**Quiero cambiar libras/dólares.**
Do you accept traveller's cheques?	**¿Acepta usted cheques de viaje?**
Can I pay with this credit card?	**¿Puedo pagar con esta tarjeta de crédito?**
How much is that?	**¿Cuánto es?**

MOSQUITOES. With the occasional exception there are rarely more
118 than a few mosquitoes at a given time, but they survive the year

round, and just one can ruin a night's sleep. Few hotels, flats or villas—anywhere on the Mediterranean—have mosquito-proofed windows. Bring your own anti-mosquito devices, whether nets, buzzers, lotions, sprays or incense-type coils that burn all night.

NEWSPAPERS and MAGAZINES *(periódico; revista)*. In major tourist areas you can buy most European and British newspapers and magazines on the day of publication. U.S. magazines are available, as well as the Paris-based *International Herald Tribune*.

The *Iberian Daily Sun*, an English-language national daily newspaper, is available on the Costa Brava, as is *Lookout*, a glossy monthly.

Have you any English-language newspapers?	**¿Tienen periódicos en inglés?**

PHOTOGRAPHY. All popular film makes and sizes are available in Spain. Prices are generally higher than in the rest of Europe or North America, so it is advisable to bring a good stock. Polaroid film is expensive.

Photo shops in major resorts can develop and print black and white or colour film in a few days at reasonable prices, and some specialize in 1-hour service.

The Spanish films, *Negra* and *Valca* in black and white, and *Negra-color* in colour, are of good quality and cheaper than the internationally known brands.

Photo shops sell lead-coated plastic bags which protect films from X-rays at airport security checkpoints.

I'd like a film for this camera.	**Quisiera un carrete para esta máquina.**
a black-and-white film	**un carrete en blanco y negro**
a colour-slide film	**un carrete de diapositivas**
a film for colour pictures	**un carrete para película en color**
35-mm film	**un carrete treinta y cinco**
super-8	**super ocho**
How long will it take to develop (and print) this film?	**¿Cuánto tardará en revelar (y sacar copias de) este carrete?**
May I take a picture?	**¿Puedo sacar una foto?**

P POLICE (*policía*). There are three police forces in Spain. The most famous are the *Guardia Civil* (Civil Guard). Each sizeable town also has *Policía Municipal* (municipal police), who wear blue or grey uniforms with badges. The third unit, the *Cuerpo Nacional de Policía,* a national anti-crime unit, can be recognized by their blue-and-white uniforms. Actually, all three forces are armed.

If you need police assistance, you can call on any one of the three.

Where's the nearest police station?	**¿Dónde está la comisaría más cercana?**

PUBLIC HOLIDAYS (*fiesta*)

January 1	*Año Nuevo*	New Year's Day
January 6	*Epifanía*	Epiphany
March 19	*San José*	St. Joseph's Day
May 1	*Día del Trabajo*	Labour Day
July 25	*Santiago Apóstol*	St. James's Day
August 15	*Asunción*	Assumption
October 12	*Día de la Hispanidad*	Discovery of America Day (Columbus Day)
November 1	*Todos los Santos*	All Saints' Day
December 6	*Día de la Constitución Española*	Constitution Day
December 25	*Navidad*	Christmas Day
Movable dates:	*Jueves Santo*	Maundy Thursday
	Viernes Santo	Good Friday
	Lunes de Pascua	Easter Monday (Catalonia only)
	Corpus Christi	Corpus Christi
	Inmaculada Concepción	Immaculate Conception (normally December 8)

These are only the national holidays of Spain. There are many special holidays for different branches of the economy or different regions. Consult the tourist office where you are staying.

120 Are you open tomorrow?	**¿Está abierto mañana?**

RADIO and TV *(radio; televisión)*. Occasional English-language broadcasts can be picked up from Majorca. Up-to-date details can be supplied by tourist-information offices. English broadcasts can also be picked up on the BBC World Service with medium-wave transistors.

RELIGIOUS SERVICES *(servicio religioso)*. In Costa Brava resort towns, religious services in English are held only occasionally. English-language mass is said at Sta. Cristina Church in Lloret. In Barcelona, Catholic and Protestant services are held in foreign languages, and there is also a synagogue and a mosque. In Barcelona Cathedral, confessions are heard each Sunday in English.

TIME DIFFERENCES. Spanish time coincides with most of Western Europe—Greenwich Mean Time plus one hour. In spring, another hour is added for Daylight Saving Time (Summer Time).

Summer Time chart:

New York	London	**Madrid**	Jo'burg	Sydney	Auckland
6 a.m.	11 a.m.	**noon**	1 p.m.	8 p.m.	10 p.m.

What time is it?   **¿Qué hora es?**

TIPPING. Since a service charge is normally included in hotel and restaurant bills, tipping is not obligatory. However, it's appropriate to tip porters, bellboys, etc. for their efforts. Follow the chart below for rough guide-lines.

Hotel porter, per bag	50 ptas.
Maid, for extra services	100–200 ptas.
Waiter	10% (optional)
Taxi driver	10%
Tourist guide	10%
Hairdresser	10%
Lavatory attendant	25–50 ptas.

Keep the change.   **Déjelo para usted.**

T   **TOILETS.** There are many expressions for "toilets" in Spanish: *aseos,* *servicios, W.C., water* and *retretes.* The first two terms are the more common.

Public toilets are to be found in most large Spanish towns, but rarely in villages. However, just about every bar and restaurant has a toilet available for public use. It's considered polite to buy a coffee or a glass of wine if you drop in specifically to use the conveniences.

Where are the toilets?   **¿Dónde están los servicios?**

TOURIST-INFORMATION OFFICES *(oficina de turismo[e]).* Spanish National Tourist Offices are maintained in many countries throughout the world:

Canada: 60 Bloor St. West, Suite 201, Toronto, Ont. M4W 3B8; tel.: (416) 961-3131.

United Kingdom: 57–58, St. James's St., London SW1 A1LD; tel.: (01) 499 09 01.

U.S.A.: 845 N. Michigan Ave., Chicago, IL 60611; tel.: (312) 944-0215.
4800 The Galleria, 5085 Westheimer Road, Houston, TX 77056; tel.: (713) 840-7411.
8383 Wilshire Boulevard, Suite 960, Beverly Hills, Los Angeles, CA 90211; tel.: (213) 658-7188/93.
665 5th Ave., New York, NY 10022; tel.: (212) 759-8822.
Casa del Hidalgo, Hypolita & St. George Streets, St. Augustine, FL 31084; tel.: (904) 829-6460.
1 Hallidie Plaza, Suite 801, San Francisco, CA 94102; tel.: (415) 346-8100.

These offices will supply you with a wide range of colourful and informative brochures and maps in English on the various towns and regions in Spain. They will also let you consult a copy of the master directory of hotels in Spain, listing all facilities and prices.

All major cities and resorts in Spain have tourist-information offices. Normal hours: 10 a.m.–1 p.m. and 4–7.30 p.m.

Barcelona: At the airport, at the central railway station (Estació de Sants), at the Estació de França (in the harbour), in Plaça de Sant Jaume (Gothic Quarter) and at Gran Via de les Corts Catalanes, 658.

Girona: Carrer Ciutadans, 12, and at the railway station.

Lloret de Mar: Plaça de la Vila.

122   Where is the tourist office?   **¿Dónde está la oficina de turismo?**

TRANSPORT

Bus services. The Costa Brava, Girona, Barcelona and inland towns of Catalonia are well served by several private bus companies. Destinations are clearly marked on the front of the bus. Remember that when taking a local bus, you normally enter by the front door.

In Barcelona, most buses for towns and resorts on the Costa Brava leave from Passeig de Colom, 3, in the harbour.

Buses are cheaper than trains, and a two-way bus ticket will work out cheaper than a travel-agency tour.

Taxis *(taxi)*. Girona and Barcelona taxis have meters, but in villages they don't, so it's a good idea to check the fare before you get in. If you take a long trip—e.g. between two villages—you will be charged a two-way fare whether you make the return journey or not.

Trains. While local trains are very slow, stopping at almost all stations, long-distance services, especially the *Talgo* and *Ter,* are fast and punctual. Tickets can be purchased at travel agencies as well as at railway stations *(estació[n] de ferrocarril)*.

In Barcelona, trains to resorts on the Costa Brava use the Cercanías station, a separate installation behind the Estació de França in the harbour.

EuroCity (EC)	International express, first and second classes
Talgo, Intercity, Electrotren, Ter, Tren Estrella	Luxury, first and second classes; supplementary charge over regular fare
Expreso, Rápido	Long-distance expresses, stopping at main stations only; supplementary charge
Omnibus, Tranvía, Automotor	Local trains, with frequent stops, usually second class only
Auto Expreso	Car train
coche cama	Sleeping-car with 1-, 2- or 3-bed compartments, washing facilities
coche comedor	Dining-car

T When's the best train to …?   **¿Cuál es el mejor tren para …?**

single (one-way)   **ida**
return (round-trip)   **ida y vuelta**
first/second   **primera/segunda**
I'd like to make seat reservations.   **Quiero reservar asientos.**

W **WATER** *(agua)*. When Spaniards drink water, it is almost invariably bottled water, rather than from the tap. If you're particularly sensitive to a change in water, you may want to follow suit. Both still (non-carbonated) and fizzy (carbonated) varieties are available.

a bottle of mineral water   **una botella de agua mineral**
    fizzy   **con gas**
    still   **sin gas**
Is this drinking water?   **¿El agua es potable?**

DAYS OF THE WEEK

Sunday	**domingo**	Wednesday	**miércoles**
Monday	**lunes**	Thursday	**jueves**
Tuesday	**martes**	Friday	**viernes**
		Saturday	**sábado**

MONTHS

January	**enero**	July	**julio**
February	**febrero**	August	**agosto**
March	**marzo**	September	**septiembre**
April	**abril**	October	**octubre**
May	**mayo**	November	**noviembre**
June	**junio**	December	**diciembre**

SOME USEFUL EXPRESSIONS

yes/no	**sí/no**
please/thank you	**por favor/gracias**
excuse me/you're welcome	**perdone/de nada**
where/when/how	**dónde/cuándo/cómo**
how long/how far	**cuánto tiempo/a qué distancia**
yesterday/today/tomorrow	**ayer/hoy/mañana**
day/week/month/year	**día/semana/mes/año**
left/right	**izquierda/derecha**
up/down	**arriba/abajo**
good/bad	**bueno/malo**
big/small	**grande/pequeño**
cheap/expensive	**barato/caro**
hot/cold	**caliente/frío**
old/new	**viejo/nuevo**
open/closed	**abierto/cerrado**
here/there	**aquí/allí**
free (vacant)/occupied	**libre/ocupado**
early/late	**temprano/tarde**
easy/difficult	**fácil/difícil**

Does anyone here speak English?	**¿Hay alguien aquí que hable inglés?**
What does this mean?	**¿Qué quiere decir esto?**
I don't understand.	**No comprendo.**
Please write it down.	**Escríbamelo, por favor.**
Is there an admission charge?	**¿Se debe pagar la entrada?**
Waiter!/Waitress!	**¡Camarero!/¡Camarera!**
I'd like …	**Quisiera …**
How much is that?	**¿Cuánto es?**
Have you something less expensive?	**¿Tiene algo más barato?**
Help me, please.	**Ayúdeme, por favor.**
Get a doctor, quickly.	**¡Llamen a un médico, rápidamente!**

125

Index

An asterisk (*) next to a page number indicates a map reference. Where there is more than one set of page references, the one in bold type refers to the main entry. For index to Practical Information, see inside front cover.

INDEX

HINTS ON COOKERY

FROM THE VICTORIANS

CONSTANCE MOORE

summersdale

Apple pie, To make

Pare, core, and quarter the apples;
boil the cores and parings in sugar
and water; strain off the liquor,
adding more sugar; grate the rind of
a lemon over the apples, and squeeze
the juice into the syrup; mix half a
dozen cloves with the fruit, put in a
piece of butter the size of a walnut;
cover with puff-pastry.

Apricots stewed in syrup, To make

Wipe the down from young
apricots, whose bloom is just
showing, and stew them as gently
as possible in a pre-prepared
syrup made of four ounces of
sugar to half a pint of water,
boiled the usual time.

BACON, TO DISTINGUISH QUALITY OF

Bacon should have a thin rind, and the fat should be firm and tinged red by the curing; the flesh should be of a clear red, without intermixture of yellow, and it should firmly adhere to the bone.

Boiling over, To prevent

Grease the inner rim of the
kettle or saucepan to the depth
of one inch from the top with
plenty of vegetable oil, and the
contents will not boil over.

Bread jam, To make

Take five slices of toasted bread,
without crusts, and place them
in four pints of boiling water
mixed with a few slices of lemon.
Then wait until it becomes a
thick jam before straining and
adding optional sweeteners.
If the bitterness of lemon is
too strong, try using wine and
sugar to spice the jam instead.

Cakes, To keep moist

Keep an apple in the cake
box to prevent the cake from
drying. Change whenever
the fruit becomes withered
or shows signs of decay.

CARBONATE OF SODA, USES FOR

A pinch added to greens will make them cook a good colour; added to milk while boiling will prevent it curdling.

CELEBRITIES, THE UNUSUAL FOOD HABITS OF

Prince Edward's favourite morning snack is hot turtle soup. This follows his usual breakfast of milk, eggs, bacon, toast with butter, fish and chicken. Following a twelve-course meal he is known to have a habit of taking a cold roast chicken to bed for fear of becoming peckish during the night.

If one has an adventurous appetite, similar to the well-known eccentric Dr William Buckland, it is encouraged to familiarise the taste buds to a world of bizarre foods, such as elephants' trunks, bats' urine and – if one can get one's hands on it – the mummified heart of King Louis XIV.

CHAMPAGNE, TO COOL

There is nothing more gratifying at a dinner party than cold champagne. To cool down in the correct way: Lay the bottle down in a basin, break up a handful of ice, put it on the bottle, sprinkle it with a little salt, and cover it with a wet piece of flannel.

CHILDREN'S FOOD, HINTS ON

We ought to be cautious, and not upon any account to allow a child pastry, confectionery, cheese, heavy dishes made of boiled or baked flours, onions, horseradish, mustard, smoked and salted meat, especially pork, and all compound dishes, for the most simple food is the most salubrious.

CHRISTMAS PUDDING, TO ADD TO

To surprise your guests on Christmas Day, follow Queen Victoria's lead and add some coins to the mixture. Queen Victoria did this as a way to say 'thank you' to her cook, but this gesture can be a 'thank you' to your guests for visiting.

THE COOK, THE DUTIES OF

The duties of a cook depend greatly upon the scale of establishments to which she belongs. In the case of a professed cook, the elementary portion of the cooking, the plain cooking, and all that relates to cleaning and scouring in kitchen, scullery, larder, and passages, and cooking utensils, is done by the kitchen and scullery maids, and only the cooking proper is the duty of this class of cook. All ingredients are prepared for her use, and the kitchen maids wait upon her and act under her orders.

Cookery, To excel in

Cookery is one of the Arts.
Those who would excel in
it must, like other artists,
be educated for it.

———— • ————

If you persevere you will soon
become skilful, and after a
time you will be able to cook.
As long as you live, you, and
those whom you love, will
never be dependent on others
for the comforts of home.

No one can learn to be a cook by reading papers on cookery any more than they can satisfy their hunger by looking at a sirloin of beef.

CREAM, To whip quickly

Pour into a glass jar and when
half full tie a parchment cover
over to make it airtight; then
shake the cream vigorously.

Cucumbers, To preserve

To preserve cucumbers from over-ripening, slice them down the middle and remove all the seeds. Then lay them in a saltwater solution, bearing an egg on the top, for three days. After, they must be boiled with water and a small lump of alum until tender; then drained; and a thin syrup to be poured over them. Leave the cucumbers in the syrup for two days and repeat twice more. This is a most time-effective method that will produce no less than perfect results.

CURRIED EGGS, TO MAKE

Slice two onions and fry them
in butter, add a tablespoonful of
curry powder; let them stew in
a pint of good broth till quite
tender; mix a cup of cream, and
thicken with arrowroot or rice
flour. Let the mixture simmer for
a few minutes, then add six to
eight hard-boiled eggs cut into
slices; heat them thoroughly,
but do not let them boil.

CUSTARD, TO MAKE SMOOTH

When soft custard or custard
sauce curdles in making, set
it in a pan of cold water and
beat with an egg-beater until
smooth. Custard that looks
honeycombed has been baked
or boiled too quickly.

DINING DUTIES,
QUEEN VICTORIA'S

Queen Victoria is renowned for her strict time-keeping and scrupulous organisation. This presents particular challenges when serving food in the royal palace. The cooks are instructed that 'trays must be kept level so that there is no spilling of gravy or sauces' – a problematic issue at Windsor Castle, where every dish has to be carried up narrow stairs from the Great Kitchen to the State Apartments.

———— • ————

To salvage any disasters, the chefs always make twenty extra dishes for each course served.

DINNER PARTY, RULES OF THE

Servants should wait at the table in clean white gloves: there are few things more disagreeable than the thumb of a clumsy waiter in your plate.

———◆·—◆———

It is essential that a dinner party opens with a selection of entrées. To match that of the guests of the Prince Regent at Brighton's Royal Pavilion on 15 January 1817, at least thirty-seven entrées must be served.

A typical Ascot Party menu

Salade de Homard
Saumon, Sauce Raifort glacé
Boeuf rôti
Pâté de Poularde et Pigeon
Poulets rôtis
Langues de Boeuf
Asperges Marinés
Côtelettes à la Connaught

Sandwiches variés

Méringues à la Crème
Bouchées Pralinées
Éclairs au Chocolat

Fraises et Crème

GLACES
Crème de Fraises
Eau de Limon
Limonade

Thé et café

Gâteaux et biscuits

Eels, To stun

It has been widely claimed that an eel is the hardest living animal to kill. Therefore, before cooking, it is most ethical to hit the head of the eel onto a block or hard table until they appear to be stunned. Then proceed with the standard gutting procedure.

Eels, To gut

First cut the skin round the neck and with some leverage pull the skin apart from the body. Then open the belly to remove of its insides and make sure any bristles that run up the back have been removed.

Eels, jellied, To make

Take one kilogram of eels and prepare them as shown above. Place in boiling water with one chopped onion, a bay leaf, the juice of half a lemon, a sprig of parsley, three crushed peppercorns and a dash of salt, pepper, vinegar and nutmeg. Take two eggs, separate the whites from the yolks, and crush and sprinkle the egg shells into the pan. Cook for fifteen minutes until the eels are tender and remove them from the pan, leaving the other ingredients to simmer. Then strain the stock through a fine sieve back into the saucepan and whisk the two egg whites into the water, leaving it to simmer for two minutes. Once cool cut the eels into chunks of two centimetres, place them into ramekins and pour the cooled stock over them. Place in the pantry to set.

Eggs, To preserve

Take a solution of gum arabic and liberally brush onto the eggs, leaving until dry. Afterwards, to prevent them being affected by contrasts in temperature, pack them up into dry charcoal dust.

Eggs, Versatility of

When good, fresh eggs are at hand they can quickly be transformed into an agreeable dish. There are said to be six hundred different ways of serving an egg.

Fast-food, Hints on

Perrier water, canned soup, canned pork & beans, Tabasco sauce, Gulden's Mustard and Folgers coffee are just a handful of the ready-available foods in stores. These are some of the best alternatives to home-made food when in a state of urgency or idleness.

Food, Ways to save money on

Before you go to market, look
over your larder and consider
well what things are wanting
– especially on a Saturday.
No well-regulated family can
suffer a disorderly caterer to
be jumping in and out to make
purchases on a Sunday morning.

Mothers, in order to stretch your
limited food sources, implore
your children to chew very
carefully and slowly and they will
therefore require much less food.

Food names, Derivation of

The gizzard and rump, or legs etc. of a dressed turkey, capon or goose; or mutton or veal kidney, scored, peppered, salted and broiled, sent up for a relish, being made very hot, has obtained the name of a 'Devil'.

In Indonesia, a root plant has been discovered that shares an uncanny resemblance with lambs. There has been much debate over whether it is in fact an animal or a plant, but with careful examination the conclusion is with that of a plant. It has been officially named the 'lamb-vegetable'.

FRENCH AND ENGLISH CHEFS, THE CULINARY BATTLE BETWEEN

When recruiting for the position of a home chef, it is most encouraged to hire someone who is French; however, an Englishman who has been trained in France will suffice.

We English are continually being told how very much better the French cook their food; but at any rate we may pride ourselves on this: They do not roast meat so well as we.

We cannot wonder that English cooks do not make good salads, for it is only the few English people who have been 'educated up to them' who care to eat salads when they are made.

The cooking, if it is fashionable, will be French, and so it follows that the language of the menu will be French also, unless one wishes to produce a very jarring effect in their guests.

Fruit, To judge the quality of

The best flavoured fruit cannot be determined by the colour of the skins, but by the size. Short, thick bananas are the best.

Green vegetables, The medicinal value of

Green vegetables contain such valuable medicinal properties that, according to eminent authorities, many of the diseases from which we suffer would be unknown were greens eaten in salad form all the year, instead of being robbed of their precious salts through being boiled in the orthodox wasteful way.

GRUEL, THE USES OF

Gruel is a thing almost gone out of fashion now, and the young ladies of the present day will entitle themselves to much gratitude if they will re-introduce the delicious, creamy – one may almost say elegant – gruel, which our grandmothers prepared for their invalids.

HAM, TO JUDGE THE STATE OF

To judge the state of ham, plunge a knife into the bone; on drawing it back, if particles of meat adhere to it, or if the smell is disagreeable, the curing has not been effectual, and the ham is not good; it should, in such a state, be immediately cooked.

Herbs, To dry for winter use

Gather your herbs from the garden
on a very dry day, as dampness will
affect their colour. They should
be freed from all dust and dirt,
and divided into small bunches
with their roots cut off. Put them
in the oven or in front of the fire
to quickly dry, but be careful not
to burn them. Then tie them in
paper bags and store in a dry place.

Herbs, To store

Parsley stored in water will turn yellow. As an effective alternative, put the herb in an airtight jar and store in a cool place.

———— • ————

Roll celery in brown paper sprinkled with water, wrap in a damp cloth and then store in a cool place to keep fresh. Before serving, submerge the celery in cold water and then let it stand for an hour to improve its crispness.

———— • ————

Between the months of July and September is the most advisable time to store herbs for winter use.

HOME-MADE BREAD,
TO PREPARE AND SERVE

One great secret of good bread-making is good kneading and plenty of elbow grease.

At dinner, where common household bread is used, it should never be cut less than an inch and a half thick. There is nothing more plebeian than *thin* bread at dinner.

———•———

KITCHEN,
THE CONDITIONS OF THE

It is essential that the kitchen is situated in the basement, or as far away from the main rooms as possible, so that the smells of cooking cannot be discovered by the family.

'The kitchen must no longer be *sanctum sanctorum*, into which even the mistress cannot enter without being considered as an impertinent intruder, and liable to the sauciness of those whose grand secret is to become the domestic tyrants, in whatever comes within the scope of their management.'

Mrs Beeton's Book of Household Management, 1861

LETTUCE, TO DRY QUICKLY

After washing thoroughly, put the lettuce in a cheesecloth bag or wire basket, and swing in a large circle for a moment or two. The water is thrown off the leaves by centrifugal force and absorbed.

MEAT, TO PREPARE

The superior pieces of meat are
generally chosen for roasting.
The coarser parts are reserved
for stewing.

———— • ————

Some cooks think it necessary
to wash meat before putting
it down. If the joint has been
bought from a respectable
dealer and has not been roughly
handled, it is most undesirable
that this should be done, as
nothing draws the goodness out
of meat more than washing it.

The time that meat should be kept must depend upon the weather and the time of year. In cold, dry weather a leg of mutton can be hung for three weeks with advantage. In hot, and particularly in what is called 'muggy' weather, it will not keep for as many days.

When meat is hanging, change its position frequently, to equally distribute the juices.

MEAT, TO COOK

If meat is to be roasted before
an open range, the fire must
be looked after fully an hour
before the meat is put down.

———————

To roast meat on a spit evenly
and without having to distract
one from other duties, use
a dog to turn the device by
linking it to a treadmill. This
is a most efficient method.

MILK LEMONADE, TO MAKE

Take a pint of boiling water
and dissolve three quarters
of loaf sugar. Then mix
them with one gill of lemon
juice, one gill of sherry and
three gills of cold milk. Stir
thoroughly and then strain to
make perfect milk lemonade.

Mother Eve's Pudding

If you would have a good
pudding, observe what you're
taught:
Take two pennyworth of eggs,
when twelve for the groat;
And of the same fruit that Eve
had once chosen,
Well pared and well chopp'd, at
least half-a-dozen;
Six ounces of bread (let your
maid eat the crust),
The crumbs must be grated as
small as the dust;

Six ounces of currants from the
stones you must sort,
Lest they break out your teeth,
and spoil all your sport;
Six ounces of sugar won't make it
too sweet;
Some salt and some nutmeg will
make it complete,
Three hours let it boil, without
hurry or flutter,
And then serve it up, without
sugar or butter.

Multicultural food and drink, The increase of

Although the rise of the Empire has brought with it an array of awful consequences, one advantage, though not redeemable in any way, has been the increase of foreign food. For example, we have adopted tea from the Chinese – it is not quintessentially British, as one may assume – and we have also acquired cooking with spices from India.

Mushroom ketchup, To make

Take a large quantity of chopped, salted mushrooms and leave to marinate for two nights. Following this, strain the excess liquid from the mushrooms and boil in a pan adding black pepper, sliced ginger, shallots and horseradish. Once liquefied and cooled, store the ketchup in a container to be used before the expiry date, which is around three years. This condiment is best served with robust meats and game.

Nice plum cake, To make

Take of flour, one pound; bi-carbonate of soda, quarter of an ounce; butter, six ounces; loaf sugar, six ounces; currants, six ounces; three eggs; milk, about four ounces; bake one hour and a half in a tin or pan.

Off meat, To freshen

Meat that has been left in a hot place for too long, or appears to be tainted, should be cooked in a boiling pot, together with a few pieces of charcoal to eradicate any germs or disease that may have propagated.

Onions, To prevent
the smell of

After peeling an onion, wash both hands in some mustard-water to prevent the smell of it lingering throughout the day.

The leaves of parsley dashed with vinegar will effectively clear the disagreeable consequences of eating an onion.

Pests, Ways to control

Use powdered resin or a solution of bitter aloes before sowing your peas to prevent any mice from touching them.

A number of corks must be cut down as thin as sixpences, and stewed in grease, and then placed in the way of the rats. They will greedily devour this special recipe, and will die of indigestion.

RANCID BUTTER, To RESTORE

To restore rancid butter, melt it in a water-bath mixed with some coarsely powdered animal charcoal (which has been thoroughly sifted from dust), and strain through a flannel.

Red meats, To prepare

Red meats, that is, beef and mutton and game – should be hung for a while before they are roasted, for only when this is done can it be expected that they will be tender.

Salad, The universality of

All cooked vegetables, every kind of meat and fish, and almost every sort of green meat that is good for food can be converted into salad.

Sausages, To make

To make sausages as were served
to Queen Victoria, finely chop
one pound of pork, one pound
of lean veal, and one pound
of beef suet, making sure that
there is no skin or gristle. Mix
together with half a pound of
breadcrumbs, the rind of a lemon
and a small grated nutmeg.
Wash and finely chop six sage
leaves, add to the mixture,
and either put into skins, or
form into little cakes, which
should be floured and fried.

Sausages, To prevent
the skin bursting

If boiled for two minutes before
being fried, sausages will cook
without bursting the skin.

Seafood, To judge
THE FRESHNESS OF

Mackerel must be perfectly fresh, or it is a very indifferent fish; it will neither bear carriage, nor being kept many hours out of the water.

———————•———————

The flavour and excellence of salmon depends upon its freshness, and the shortness of time since it was caught; for no method can completely preserve the delicate flavour it has when just taken out of the water.

Prawns and shrimps, when fresh, are firm and crisp.

To tell if oysters are fresh, the shell should be firmly closed; when the shells of oysters are opened, they are dead, and unfit for food.

SHEEP'S HEAD, TO COOK

To cook a sheep's head, first cut out the brain and the tongue from the head and be sure to wash these both with care. Then, dissect the head into two; at the same time remove the eyes and gristle from the inside of the nose. Again, rinse the head thoroughly. In the meantime, bring a pot of salted water to the boil and add the brain along with two large onions and three large carrots into the mix. Leave to boil for fifteen minutes and serve the head with the boiled onions and carrots on the side.

Sheep's brain with matelote sauce, To cook

Detach six sheep's brains from the heads, ensuring that they do not sever in the process, and put them in a pan of warm water for two hours. Then place them in a saucepan filled with boiling water and a dash of salt and vinegar. Once firmed, take them out of the boiling water and put in very cold water immediately. Mix with three slices of bacon, one onion, two cloves, parsley and a seasoning of salt and pepper in a pan of boiling water and simmer for twenty-five minutes.

THE SICK, FOOD FOR

'Sick people do not like their soup, tea, or other drinks spilt into the saucer, nor to return to an old piece of jelly or pudding which they have not been able to finish. All that they have tasted should be at once removed, and fresh brought in when required. Arabella Plumptre testifies that "Wines should never be given to invalids without the expressed permission of their medical attendant, as they are dangerous medicines and do more harm than good."'

Domestic Management: The Healthful Cookery Book, 1810

Soup, Assumptions about

One seems to have an idea
that soup, if it is to be worth
anything, must be made from
meat. And yet some very
excellent and nourishing and
most palatable soups can be
made without it.

Sponge cake, Queen Victoria's, To make

Take equal weight of eggs and sugar; half their weight in sifted flour; to twelve eggs, add the grated rind of three lemons, and the juice of two. Beat the eggs carefully, white and yolk separately, before they are used. Stir the materials thoroughly together, and bake in a quick oven. This delicate cake has come to be known as the 'Victoria Sponge' cake, given to Queen Victoria's preference of a slice with her cup of tea in the afternoon.

SPONGE CAKE, TO ICE

Beat together half a pound of
icing sugar, the whites of two
eggs and a dash of orange flower
water, and bake, then while
the cake is still warm, pour the
icing over evenly. Ornament
with fruit and put in the oven
to harden, but not to colour.

STALE BREAD, TO FRESHEN

To refresh stale bread to an edible
state simply put the necessary
amount in the oven and heat until
it is hot throughout. This method
will also help preserve the bread
before it ages.

STOMACH ACHES AND UNEASE, TO PREVENT

Serve a sorbet flavoured with port, brandy or rum to cool and prepare the stomach for courses of a substantial size and richness.

STRAWBERRY-WATER ICE, TO MAKE

Take one large pottle of scarlet strawberries, the juice of a lemon, a pound of sugar or one pint of strong syrup, and half a pint of water. Mix, first rubbing the fruit through a sieve, and freeze.

THICK SOUP, CRITICISM ON

There are various indictments
against any sort of thick soup.
Nearly all true gastronomes
prefer a consommé to a
thick preparation for the
commencement of the principal
meal of the day. It is only
the aldermanic digestion
which can satisfactorily
cope with a thick soup.

THIEVES, TO STOP

Despite the servants' help around the house they are largely known to pilfer as many goods as possible without being suspected. To prevent any high-quality meat going astray remember to lock it in the meat safe after cooking.

Tongue and brain pudding, To make

Skin and wash the tongues and brains of four sheep. Slice them into thin pieces and alternate the slices of each in a pudding basin, adding salt, pepper, chopped onion and parsley with each layer. Place a sliced hard-boiled egg on the top layer and pour over a teaspoon of flour and quarter of a pint of milk that has been mixed thoroughly. Place on the top crust and boil for three hours. A young sliced cucumber is a good accompaniment to serve with this dish.

White meats, To prepare

White meats, such as lamb, veal and pork, taint quickly, and require to be roasted when fresh.

WOMEN IN THE KITCHEN

'A real lady is not ashamed to
have it known that she goes into
the kitchen; on the contrary, it
is more likely that she will be
a little proud of being thought
capable of superintending
the preparing of the feast.'

The Lady's Book of Manners, 1890

'If only English girls would give time, care, and forethought to cookery in their own homes, we should have many a father and brother strong and hearty who now looks white and delicate; we should have less waste in our kitchens, less bad temper in our families, and, I really believe, more thankfulness in our hearts.'

———— • ————

'Things done hurriedly are generally done badly. It is my conviction that the time which a girl devotes to cookery is well and wisely spent.'

'I have always thought that there is no more fruitful source of family discontent than a housewife's badly-cooked dinners and untidy ways. Men are now so well served out of doors – at their clubs, well-ordered taverns, and dining-houses – that in order to compete with the attractions of these places, a mistress must be thoroughly acquainted with the theory and practice of cookery, as well as be perfectly conversant with all the other arts of making and keeping a comfortable home.'

Mrs Beeton's Book of Household Management, 1861

What wife can truly dread the
kitchen when she is possessed of
a mixing and whisk machine?
There are many little variations
of the device to suit a lady's
capriciousness and all capable
of reducing egg mixture
and batter to incomparable
lightness with but a few
revolutions of the handle.

Yeast, To prepare

Boil one pound of good flour, a quarter pound of brown sugar and a little salt in two gallons of water, for one hour. When milk is warm, bottle it, and cork it closed. Once twenty-four hours has passed it will be fit for use.

Yorkshire cream cheese, To make

Take a substantial amount of cream and tie it in a piece of wet cloth where it should be stored in a cool place for seven or eight days. Then remove from the cloth and put into a mould and leave again for another two to three days. Keep turning twice a day until the cream cheese is ready for use.

Yorkshire puddings, To make

Mix together six large
tablespoons of flour and a
saltspoonful of salt, and add
milk in small quantities until the
mixture becomes a stiff batter.
When there are no lumps in the
mixture, add the remainder of
the one and a half pints of milk,
and three eggs, which should be
well beaten. Mix together and
pour into a shallow tin that has
already been greased with beef
dripping. Cook the pudding
in the oven for an hour and a
half, placed under the meat to
catch its dripping gravies.

HINTS ON HEALTH

FROM THE VICTORIANS

CONSTANCE MOORE

HINTS ON HEALTH FROM
THE VICTORIANS

Constance Moore

ISBN: 978 1 84953 244 0   Hardback   £3.99

*To ease the pain of teething,
hang a dead mole around
the neck of your baby…*

For tips on how to treat earache, avoid being flustered by flu and curb the torment of blistered feet, look no further than this miscellany of hints on health from the Victorians.

www.summersdale.com